"Don Gossett is gifted in his ability to communicate the benefits of confessing the Word of God."

—*Pastor Holmes Williams, D.D.*,
The People's Cathedral,
Barbados

"This book, like Don Gossett's previous writings, will ignite the spark of faith within us to trust Jesus for all of our needs."

—*Reverend Dr. Jerry Lynn*,
Reach Out Fellowship,
Albany, New York

"Don's wisdom, experience, and revelation have been some of the greatest blessings in my life."

—*Pastor Glen Curry*,
Pillars of Faith Christian Center,
Industry, California

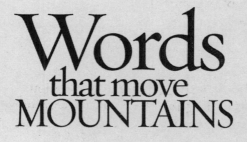

Words
that move
MOUNTAINS

Words
that move
MOUNTAINS

E. W. KENYON &
DON GOSSETT

WHITAKER
HOUSE

WORDS THAT MOVE MOUNTAINS

Revised and Expanded Edition of *The Power of Spoken Faith*

Don Gossett
P.O. Box 2
Blaine, Washington 98231
www.dongossett.com

ISBN: 978-1-60374-082-1
Printed in the United States of America
© 2003, 2009 by Don Gossett

Whitaker House
1030 Hunt Valley Circle
New Kensington, PA 15068
www.whitakerhouse.com

3 4 5 6 7 8 9 10 11 ᴜᴡ 16 15 14 13 12 11 10

ACKNOWLEDGMENTS

Let me introduce to you several people who exemplify the true spirit of generosity.

First and foremost is Dr. E. W. Kenyon. It was the passion of his life to share with others what God had taught him through the Word. He diligently applied himself to writing sixteen books, editing hundreds of magazines, and creating Bible study courses and gospel tracts. What a giving heart he demonstrated!

Second, before Dr. Kenyon passed away in 1948, he asked his daughter, Ruth, to keep the work going. For fifty years, Ruth was faithful to do so. She shared with me many times how fulfilling it was to see and know the effectiveness of her father's writings—literally all over the globe.

Next, I am pleased to commend the excellent work of Pastor Joe McIntyre, who now serves as president of Kenyon's Gospel Publishing Society. When books were published presenting "unfair and unscholarly" attacks on the writings of Dr. Kenyon, Joe felt compelled to write an apologetic thesis, which he presented to his church family.

I admire Joe McIntyre for his labor of love in investing hundreds of hours of research and authoring the book *E. W. Kenyon and His Message of Faith: The True Story*.

Last, Charisma House, owned by my dear friend Stephen Strang, generously gave me permission to include materials from Pastor McIntyre's aforementioned book here in *Words That Move Mountains*.

My special thanks go to Dr. T. L. Osborn, Tulsa, Oklahoma, for his contributions toward this book.

I also owe my appreciation to Pastor Don Cox, Waterloo, Iowa, for items he has shared with me.

—*Don Gossett*

CONTENTS

INTRODUCTION

It is written: "I believed; therefore I have
spoken." With that same spirit of faith
we also believe and therefore speak.
—2 Corinthians 4:13 (NIV)

In 1952, I was given a copy of *The Wonderful Name of Jesus* by Dr. E. W. Kenyon. My study of this book was enhanced by the fact that just the year before, at an altar of prayer, I had received a startling revelation of the authority of the name of Jesus.

Wherefore God also hath highly exalted him, and given him a name which is above every name: that at the name of Jesus every knee should bow, of things in heaven, and things in earth, and things under the earth; and that every tongue should confess that Jesus Christ is Lord, to the glory of God the Father.

(Philippians 2:9–11)

Dr. Kenyon's revelation of the name of Jesus

set my soul on fire. I was ministering at tent meetings in Fresno and Modesto, California, at that time. I did daily early-morning radio broadcasts on stations in Lodi and Modesto. Driving from each city, I was flowing with an enormous appreciation of the majesty of the name. Over and over, I sang songs and choruses about the precious name.

I was soon able to make contact with Ruth Kenyon, Dr. Kenyon's daughter and head of Kenyon's Gospel Publishing Society.

During my first phone conversation with Ruth, she informed me that Dr. Kenyon had left sixteen books to posterity, which she ordered for me. She also explained that Dr. Kenyon's *In His Presence* was the book God was using most at that time.

When I received the shipment of Dr. Kenyon's sixteen books, I eagerly studied and devoured them all. Knowing the blessing *The Wonderful Name* had been to me there in California, I expected *In His Presence* would likewise ignite my heart.

However, my first reading of the book didn't achieve that for me. A few months later, while in meetings in Kansas City, I reread *In His Presence.* This time, the revelation came to my spirit. I was so caught up in His presence that I felt I was walking on fleecy clouds as I went from my hotel to the church where I was ministering.

I then realized that it was necessary for the Holy Spirit to give me revelation knowledge to grasp what Dr. Kenyon had written.

In my youthful zeal, I once said to my friends, "I so love what the Kenyon books have done for me, I think I would almost like to change my name to 'Don Kenyon' so I could be readily identified with his wonderful ministry." (Of course, I didn't make that change. I'm still Don Gossett.)

In 1954, I was back in Southern California for meetings. At that time, the Kenyon's Gospel Publishing Society offices were in Fullerton, not far from Los Angeles, where I was ministering. One day, I made an appointment to drive out to Fullerton to meet with Ruth and her mother.

It was an unforgettable experience. I said to Ruth, "I have been an avid reader and student of many books written by evangelical and Pentecostal authors. Why is it your father had the ability to open the Word with such unique authority?"

Ruth replied, "Don, if you had grown up in

my father's house, perhaps you would understand. The open Bible was all over our home.

"One of the sweetest experiences in my youth was passing by our bathroom where my father would often shave with the door ajar. He would be dressed except for his shirt. His face would be lathered to prepare for his shave. But beside the sink would be an open Bible. He couldn't keep his eyes off the Word. I would hear him rejoicing, weeping, and praising God for some nugget of truth he had read in the Scriptures."

A few years later, Ruth moved the Kenyon's Gospel Publishing Society offices back to Lynnwood, Washington, less than a hundred miles from my home in Surrey. She invited me to be a regular contributor to *Kenyon's Herald of Life,* a paper she published.

After Ruth's husband, Mr. Iams, passed away, I wrote an article entitled "Again She Stands Alone." I emphasized how Dr. Kenyon had selected Ruth to continue his ministry the very day he knew the Lord was calling him home. Dr. Kenyon's wife had joined Ruth in the ministry until the Lord called her home, also. Now, with her mother and father already gone, Mr. Iams' passing left Ruth alone.

The Reverend Norman Houseworth in

northern Alberta, Canada, read the article I wrote. His wife had died a few years earlier, and the Lord used my article to give him a nudge. He went to meet Ruth with the prospect of their being married, and that is exactly what happened.

In 1972, I requested and obtained Ruth's permission to use Kenyon's writings in my book, *The Power of Your Words*. (This book is also available through Whitaker House.) The book was about the confession of the Word and combined Dr. Keyon's excellent materials on the subject with my own recorded thoughts.

When Ruth went to be with the Lord a few years ago, the Kenyon staff gave Joe McIntyre access to writings of Dr. Kenyon that had never been released. Pastor McIntyre did excellent research and wrote his book, *E. W. Kenyon and His Message of Faith: The True Story.* I have included quotations and items from Joe McIntyre's book in this book, *Words That Move Mountains*.

Words That Move Mountains carries the same format as *The Power of Your Words*. The author of each chapter is identified beneath that chapter's title. It is my prayer that this book will bless you and encourage you to realize the power of your words spoken in faith.

PART I:
PRINCIPLES OF AFFIRMATION

– 1 –
REACHING AND TOUCHING IN FAITH

by Don Gossett

Reaching out in faith results in the most significant touch of all—the touch of God. In October 1960, my family and I moved from Tulsa, Oklahoma, to Vancouver, British Columbia, to begin a new ministry. For a year, we traveled the Canadian prairies and conducted evangelistic meetings in churches. For those twelve months, we journeyed without really having a place to call home.

My five children recall that period of time as one of the most adventurous seasons of their lives, but it wasn't easy for them. Michael and Judy slept on the backseat of our old 1956 Buick. Jeanne and Donnie slept on the floorboard. Our baby, Marisa, slept between Joyce and me in the front seat.

Having gotten a "lemon" in business matters (one that cost us the home we had owned), by the grace of God, we made lemonade.

During those months, I taught my children to memorize many verses of God's Word, and all of them delighted in the Bible stories I taught them. Michael says he memorized more than one hundred Bible verses during that time.

We enrolled the children who were old enough to attend school in the British Columbia Correspondence School, and my wife, Joyce, taught them when we were on the road.

In 1961, we decided to settle in a little motel unit in Victoria so that we could put our children in school. Things didn't go especially well with all seven of us living in two rooms. Cramped is an appropriate word to describe this time in our lives.

For five weeks that fall, I conducted meetings with Pastor Jim Nichols in a church in Longview, Washington. I received a love offering for my ministry each week. But while there was lots of love, there just wasn't much offering. One Monday, I had serious car trouble on the way home and had to use most of my love offering to pay for car repairs. There wasn't enough left over to pay the thirty dollars necessary for the rental of our little motel unit.

The embarrassment of not being able to pay the rent, along with inadequate clothes and provisions for my children, was nearly more than I could take.

I made arrangements to postpone paying the rent for a week, left Joyce what money I had for the week's groceries, and returned to my meetings in Longview.

I asked God many questions. "Why are we in such desperate need financially?" "Why did we lose our home by repossession?"

During that time, I read a wonderful book by Vernon Howard called *Word Power.* God used the message of that book to help me freshly understand the power of my words, and He gave me this Scripture: *"Can two walk together, except they be agreed?"* (Amos 3:3). God was asking me, "Do you want to walk with Me? Then you must agree with Me. You agree with Me by saying what My Word says. You have disagreed with Me by speaking lack, sickness, fear, defeat, and inability. If you want to walk with Me, you must agree with Me." As this truth became real to me, I asked His forgiveness for my failure to agree with Him and His Word.

I must not hasten away from the truth of Amos 3:3. It's in the heart of all sincere Christians to walk closely with the Lord. The Bible records the testimony of Enoch: "[He] *walked with God*" (Genesis 5:24). Enoch wasn't the only person who could walk with God; you and I also can walk with Him. Hebrews 11:5 says that Enoch *"pleased God"* by agreeing in faith with God. We can walk just as closely with God as Enoch did if we choose to agree with Him in faith.

How do we agree with God? We agree by saying what God says while disagreeing with the wicked, lying devil. (Hallelujah for such a dynamic truth!)

As a result of this realization, I began to agree with God as I had never done before. The Holy Spirit began teaching me some key Scriptures: *"Ye have wearied the LORD with your words. Yet ye say, Wherein have we wearied him?"* (Malachi 2:17).

God put His finger on the ways I had wearied Him with my words—expressing my worries and frustrations concerning my "lack of money." *"Your words have been stout against me, saith the LORD. Yet ye say, What have we spoken so much against thee?"* (Malachi 3:13).

I cried out in protest, "Lord, I would never speak against You! I love You with all my heart.

Oh, Lord, I would never, never speak against You!"

Tenderly, the Lord dealt with me. "*'Your words have been stout.'* They have been strong and defensive against Me because they have been out of harmony with My Word. You have spoken words far below the standard of My Word. You must discipline your lips so that our words will be in harmony."

As I meditated on this unusual encounter with the living God, I wrote down twelve affirmations that were to become my daily discipline. I called this list of affirmations "My Never Again List."

People have often asked me, "Why did you write this list?" I wrote it as a desperate man, seeking God's ways to overcome all the adversities, financial failures, defeats, and bondages I had known for some time. I didn't write it to impress anyone with my writing ability. It was written as a discipline of my own heart in order to let the Word of God prevail, as Acts 19:20 says, *"So mightily grew the word of God and prevailed."*

These twelve affirmations became the watchwords of my new walk with God. They became the report card by which to check my life. God's

Word in these twelve affirmations became the solid ground I stood on. They were the anchor that prevented me from sinking in a sea of failure, fear, and satanic oppression.

I could use many words to describe the impact these twelve affirmations have had on my life—words like "life-changing" and "awesome." When I wrote "My Never Again List," I wasn't thinking of the millions of people who would eventually read about this powerful discipline and experience their own transformations. I wrote it as a step in my pursuit of God.

Jesus declared that we are His disciples; a disciple is someone who disciplines himself. This list of affirmations has never been a magic formula; instead, it is a clear-cut discipline. It is putting Amos 3:3 into practice and agreeing with God in all areas of life.

I will always praise God for directing me to write down this list of affirmations. If no one else had been blessed by it, I would still praise the Lord. But, in addition to blessing me, it has been printed in many languages and distributed throughout the world. God has used it to minister to literally millions of people—people who have read it and put it into practice.

The list is founded on a passage from Romans:

But what saith it? The word is nigh thee, even in thy mouth, and in thy heart: that is, the word of faith, which we preach; that if thou shalt confess with thy mouth the Lord Jesus, and shalt believe in thine heart that God hath raised him from the dead, thou shalt be saved. For with the heart man believeth unto righteousness; and with the mouth confession is made unto salvation.   (Romans 10:8–10)

It is also in harmony with the spirit of faith, as revealed in 2 Corinthians 4:13:

We having the same spirit of faith, according as it is written, I believed, and therefore have I spoken; we also believe, and therefore speak.

"My Never Again List"

▶ Never again will I confess "I can't" for *"I can do all things through Christ which strengtheneth me"* (Philippians 4:13).

▶ Never again will I confess lack, for *"my God shall supply all* [my] *need according to his riches in glory by Christ Jesus"* (Philippians 4:19).

▶ Never again will I confess fear, for *"God hath not given us the spirit of fear; but of power, and of love, and of a sound mind"* (2 Timothy 1:7).

▶ Never again will I confess doubt and lack of

faith, for *"God hath dealt to every man the measure of faith"* (Romans 12:3).

▶ Never again will I confess weakness, for *"the Lord is the strength of my life"* (Psalm 27:1) and *"the people who know their God shall be strong, and carry out great exploits"* (Daniel 11:32 NKJV).

▶ Never again will I confess supremacy of Satan over my life, *"because greater is he that is in* [me], *than he that is in the world"* (1 John 4:4).

▶ Never again will I confess defeat, for *"God... always causeth us to triumph in Christ"* (2 Corinthians 2:14).

▶ Never again will I confess lack of wisdom, for *"Christ Jesus...has become for us wisdom from God"* (1 Corinthians 1:30 NIV).

▶ Never again will I confess the domination of sickness over my life, for *"with his stripes we are healed"* (Isaiah 53:5).

▶ Never again will I confess worries and frustrations, for I am *"casting all* [my] *care upon him; for he careth for* [me]" (1 Peter 5:7). In Christ I am "carefree."

▶ Never again will I confess bondage, for Scripture says, *"Where the Spirit of the Lord is, there is liberty"* (2 Corinthians 3:17). My body is the temple of the Holy Spirit.

▶ Never again will I confess condemnation, for *"there is therefore now no condemnation to them which are in Christ Jesus"* (Romans 8:1). I am in Christ; therefore, I am free from condemnation.

– 2 –
THAT WE MIGHT BE HEALED

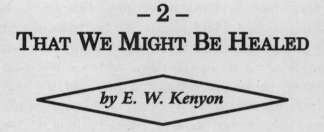

by E. W. Kenyon

I saw the first miracles of healing in my ministry in the Free Baptist Church at Springville, New York, where I was pastor.

Before this I had always been suspicious of anyone who claimed their prayers for healing were answered....I felt we had doctors and surgeons and sanitariums for that purpose. Why did we need anything else? At the time, I firmly believed that God had given us physicians and other methods of healing.

I knew nothing about the name of Jesus or that healing was part of the plan of redemption, but my heart was very hungry, and I was studying the Word diligently. I had just received the Holy Spirit. The Word had become a living thing. I had awakened faith in many hearts by my newfound love for the Word.

One day, the clerk of our church...asked me if I would pray for his wife. She had been ill for many months. I will never forget how I shrank from it. But I had to go. She lay in bed, and I prayed for her as best I knew how. I did not understand about the name of Jesus, but God in His great grace honored me, and she was instantly healed. That night, she came to church and gave her testimony. It created a great deal of sensation and some criticism. Some said it was her time to get well, anyway. A few gave credit where it belonged.

A young woman in a neighboring town was healed next. She was helpless, unable to walk. If I remember correctly, she had undergone an operation, and it had left her in a fearful condition. I prayed for her. She was healed instantly and got up and went about her work. She is now on our correspondence list.

From that day on, healings came—not many, though, for not many people asked to be prayed for. While we were holding services in Massachusetts, healings became more frequent. One day, I discovered the use of the name of Jesus. Then, miracles became a daily occurrence.

That We Might Be Healed

In our work at the tabernacle, I did not teach healing except in a very guarded way. Yet as the people began to obey the Word and to test its promises, healings and other signs followed, and I could not suppress the truth. Had I any right to hold down the truth through fear of persecution or misrepresentation when I knew that God could heal, and was healing, the sick?

The text of *That We Might Be Healed* is taken from "His Name on Our Lips Brings Healing," *Kenyon's Herald of Life*, 1 July 1941, as quoted in *E. W. Kenyon and His Message of Faith: The True Story* by Joe McIntyre (Lake Mary, FL: Charisma House, 1997), 62–63.

– 3 –
CONFESSION

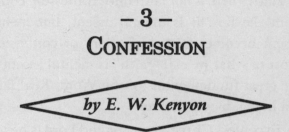

by E. W. Kenyon

Believing is utterly dependent upon confession. Believing is action. It is the verb of the life of faith. It is lifting the flood gates and letting the stream go through.

Believing is acting on the Word that God has spoken. There isn't any believing without action. There may be an assent to the fact, but scriptural belief demands action; it demands that we act before God acts.

It is not believing to act after God acts to confirm His Word. To believe and act before God has acted is the scriptural meaning of belief.

Faith is something that comes after one has acted. The relation of believing and faith to confession is fully realized.

When we say "confession," we do not mean confession of sin. We mean the confession of our faith. We confess what we have believed.

Faith, then, is not faith until confession comes from the lips. It is mental assent, but mental assent becomes faith by action, or confession. Most of what we call "faith" is mental assent to the great fundamentals of the Word. Real faith is a living, moving force.

To confess Christ as Savior and Lord is believing. To confess before the world that He is able to supply all your needs according to his riches in glory in Christ Jesus—that is believing. (See Philippians 4:19.)

You can see that there is no believing on Christ as Savior and Lord without lip confession. (See Romans 10:10.) There is no God-accepted faith that does not manifest itself in confession.

Only recently have I seen with clearness the infinite value of continual affirmation, not only to the inner man (to the soul and spirit), but also to the world.

Our spiritual lives depend upon our constant affirmation of what God has declared, what God is in Christ, and what we are to the Father in Christ. Confession is faith's confirmation. To constantly affirm the things that God is to you and you are to God, and the things you are in Christ and what Christ is in you, is to give faith the wings to reach higher altitudes in the spiritual experiences.

For example, Methodism was powerful in its early days, and those who were involved in the movement practiced a continual confession of the things for which John Wesley stood. When they stopped this verbal confession, faith stopped growing, and acting upon the promises in God's Word became more difficult.

It would be valuable for us if we could now think of a few poignant statements of fact in the Word.

In Colossians 2:10, Paul said, *"ye are complete in him."* Your heart repeats this refrain.

"I am complete in my spirit. I have partaken of His fullness, of His completeness; His completeness makes it possible for me to stand in His presence uncondemned and unafraid. His completeness makes me equal to any situation that may come upon me. I stand complete in His resurrection life. All that the Father saw in

Him, He sees in me today. I am the workmanship of God, created in Christ Jesus."

Say it over in your heart again: "I am complete in Him."

You might have physical weaknesses, but understand that the law of faith is that you confess to yourself that what God says about you is true. You do not need to have any feeling about it or experience any symptoms. The fact is that if you were healed before you confessed, it would not have been an affirmation; it would have been a confirmation. You would be simply confirming what God had done.

But now, before it takes place, you can say, *"with his stripes* [I am] *healed"* (Isaiah 53:5); not, "I may be" or "I am going to be," but "I am." That is believing; that is an act of real faith. By faith, you now stand complete in Him. What is faith to you is fact to Him.

You stand there with joy. You praise Him. You adore Him for it. You are complete in Him. Your joy is complete in Him, your rest is complete in Him, and your peace is complete in Him.

Say, *"The LORD is the strength of my life; of whom shall I be afraid?"* (Psalm 27:1). Say, "He is the strength of my body, so I can do anything that He desires done." You no longer talk about your sickness and failure because He is the strength of your life.

Life, in this case, means physical life. God is the strength of your arms and legs, of your stomach and bowels. He is the health of your navel, the center of your nerves. Where fear has come with great force and held you in bondage, He has banished it and has become your strength.

He is the strength of your mind, for you have the mind of Christ.

He is the strength of your spirit, for your spirit is the place where courage is power, where faith arises and dominates the soul, and where peace finds its home and radiates out through the faculties of the soul. Rest, peace, faith, love, and hope find their home in the spirit, and He is the strength of your spirit.

The great Christ is seated there. That is His throne, blessed be His name.

Now, you are not going to fear circumstances. You are not going to be afraid of anything, for He is the strength of your life. He is your righteousness.

I wish that everyone would truly understand what this means. It is God Himself, His holiness, His eternal righteousness, His mind. He swallows us up. He absorbs us, overwhelms us. He immerses us in Himself.

Just as the Holy Spirit came in that upper room on the day of Pentecost, filled it, and immersed every disciple in it with Himself, so the righteousness of God immerses us. As the Holy Spirit went inside each of them on the day of Pentecost and made their bodies His home, so God, by the new birth, the new creation, makes us His righteousness in Christ Jesus.

We can say without fear or any sense of unworthiness, "God is my righteousness." You glory in His righteousness. You revel in His righteousness. You make your boast. You stand up and shout His righteousness.

Then, your heart grows quiet. *For he hath made him to be sin for us, who knew no sin; that we might be made the righteousness of God in him* (2 Corinthians 5:21).

Now you know not only that He is your righteousness, but also that you are His righteousness. He said, "That He might be the

righteousness of the one who has faith in Jesus."
(See Romans 3:26.) You have faith in Jesus; He
is your righteousness, and, miracle of miracles,
you are His.

You stand complete in Him. He is the strength
of your very being. Your body has become His
home. He dwells in you.

As Paul said, *"I have been crucified with Christ
and I no longer live, but Christ lives in me"* (Galatians
2:20 NIV).

– 4 –
WE CONQUER BY CONFESSION

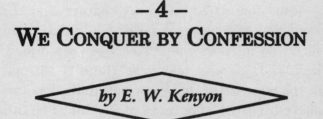

by E. W. Kenyon

Faith is the creative force in God and in the new creation. Faith is the creative ability that expresses itself only by confession. God dared to say, *"Let there be lights in the firmament of the heaven..."* (Genesis 1:14). And when He did, the universe came into being.

Jesus dared to ask for bread when a hungry crowd of thousands surrounded Him. His disciples said, *"five barley loaves, and two small fishes: but what are they among so many?"* (John 6:9).

Jesus did not answer their unbelief based in sense knowledge. He looked up to the Father and thanked Him.

The creative ability that was in Jesus is the nature of God Himself. You have the nature of

God in you through Eternal Life. You are a partaker of the divine nature (see 2 Peter 1:4); that same creative ability is in you. But it must be manifested by your confession.

Jesus dominated the laws of nature, and His word was the word of faith. Had Jesus been silent, no miracles would have been performed. Jesus said, *"Lazarus, come forth"* (John 11:43), and in the presence of that great multitude, Lazarus obeyed. There had never been anything like this resurrection before. The man had been dead for four days, and his body was decaying. Jesus dominated every law of nature; He set each of them aside.

These negative natural forces came into being when man became a subject of the devil. Jesus acted as though those laws had never been. Do you know that God has lifted each of us who is in Christ above those laws that came into being when man was made the subject of Satan?

We can say, *"I can do all things through Christ which strengtheneth me"* (Philippians 4:13); "I can meet every emergency." We read and believe 2 Corinthians 2:14: *"Now thanks be unto God, which always causeth us to triumph in Christ."*

But you say, "When Paul wrote that, wasn't he oftentimes in prison?"

Yes, but he was always a master of the prison. Do you remember when he and Silas were in the jail at Philippi? They were masters before the morning sun arose.

Do you remember the story of Peter being loosed from jail by an angel? He was a master. He did not understand this mastery because the revelation of it had not been given yet, but we have it now in the Pauline Epistles.

We know who we are, and we know that we can conquer the adversary with words. That truth thrills us.

Remember that Jesus said, *"I came down from heaven, not to do mine own will, but the will of him that sent me"* (John 6:38). He declared, *"I have not spoken of myself; but the Father which sent me, he gave me a commandment, what I should say, and what I should speak"* (John 12:49).

Can you speak God's Word to Satan? Then take your place and dare to fearlessly face the enemy. He can't stand before you. Angels are on your side. God is on your side. The living Word is on your lips. Use it. You are a conqueror.

– 5 –
DAILY AFFIRMATIONS

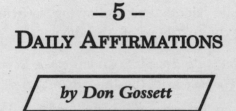

by Don Gossett

To affirm is to make firm. An affirmation is a statement of truth that you make firm by repetition. *"These things...affirm constantly"* (Titus 3:8). *"Let us hold unswervingly to the hope we profess, for he who promised is faithful"* (Hebrews 10:23 NIV). Your faith becomes effective by acknowledging every good thing that is in you in Christ Jesus. (See Philemon 6.)

The Bible includes hundreds of passages that speak about the power of words. I challenge you to speak the twenty-five affirmations that I have listed. They will be more effective as you speak them with volume, feeling, conviction, and enthusiasm. Words weakly spoken have minimal results.

I encourage you to speak some of these affirmations three to five times daily. Jesus is our primary example of how to live the Christian life, and in Matthew 26:44, "[Jesus] *prayed the third time, saying the same words.*"

Speak aloud the following affirmations during the first hour of your day:

▶ *"This is the day the LORD has made; let us rejoice and be glad in it"* (Psalm 118:24 NIV).

▶ Today I choose love instead of fear. I choose peace instead of conflict. I choose to be a love-finder instead of a faultfinder. I choose to be a love-giver instead of a love-seeker.

▶ *"I will bless the LORD at all times: his praise shall continually be in my mouth"* (Psalm 34:1).

▶ *"Let the weak say, I am strong"* (Joel 3:10). (Notice that it's the weak, not the strong, who are commanded to affirm this!)

▶ I am a woman/man of God. He has cleansed me by the blood of Christ. My Father has filled me with His Spirit. So, I am dedicated to the Lord Jesus, strong and powerful in Him. I worship and serve Him with all the divine energy He inspires within me.

▶ *"Greater is he that is in* [me], *than he that is in the world"* (1 John 4:4).

▶ I am humble, strong, courageous, full of

faith, and powerful in the Lord. (Repeat three times.)

▶ *"If God be for us, who can be against us?"* (Romans 8:31).

▶ I am a child of God. My Father has adopted me into His family. He has moved me out of darkness and into the light of His kingdom. God's protective shield is about me, and He is providing for every need in my life.

▶ *"My God shall supply all* [my] *need according to his riches in glory by Christ Jesus"* (Philippians 4:19).

▶ Every day in every way, by the grace of God, I am getting better and better through a positive attitude, spoken words of faith, and disciplined actions.

▶ *"God has not given us a spirit of fear, but of power and of love and of a sound mind"* (2 Timothy 1:7 NKJV).

▶ God has forgiven me, and I forgive myself.

▶ The anointing of the Holy One abides within me. (See 1 John 2:27.)

▶ My generous Father has blessed me with abundant life. I am grateful for this, and I enjoy giving my time, talents, money, and love to others.

▶ *"But he was wounded for our transgressions, he was bruised for our iniquities: the chastisement of our peace was upon him; and with his stripes we are healed"* (Isaiah 53:5).

▶ God loves me with an unconditional love, so I love Him with all my heart, soul, and mind. I am free to love myself, and this allows me to love my neighbor.

▶ *"[We] overcame him [Satan] by the blood of the Lamb and by the word of [our] testimony, and [we do] not love [our] lives to the death"* (Revelation 12:11 NKJV).

▶ I belong to Jesus, so I am friendly, strong, happy, and victorious. Everything is fine.

▶ *"Rejoice in the Lord alway: and again I say, Rejoice"* (Philippians 4:4).

▶ God has given me a strong body and a fine brain, and He has filled me with His Holy Spirit. This makes me a talented, gifted, persistent, and hard worker. I will reach my goals.

▶ *"The LORD is the strength of my life; of whom shall I be afraid?"* (Psalm 27:1).

Daily Affirmations

▶ God loves me, so I love Him, believe in Him, and trust my life to His care. I will serve Him faithfully!

▶ I *"cast all* [my] *anxiety on him because he cares for* [me]" (1 Peter 5:7 NIV).

▶ I feel healthy. I feel happy. I feel terrific! *"The LORD is the strength of my life"* (Psalm 27:1).

▶ God is my loving Father. He has given me a Savior, His Holy Spirit, a healthy body, a fine mind, material abundance, a beautiful world, and many friends. I am thankful! I am thankful! I am thankful!

– 6 –
My Spiritual Affirmations

by E. W. Kenyon

An affirmation is faith's confession; it is the heart singing its anthem of liberty.

"God is my righteousness."

Who is my righteousness? Romans 3:26 says, *"that he might be just, and the justifier of him which believeth in Jesus."* Christ Jesus Himself is righteous, and He is the righteousness of all who believe. This is the reality of the dream of God for humanity.

If God is my righteousness, who is he that can condemn me? Who can bring me under condemnation? Who can rob me of my fellowship? (See Romans 8:34–37.) God has declared that *"there is therefore now no condemnation to them which are in Christ Jesus"* (Romans 8:1).

"I am in Christ Jesus."

Jesus was made righteousness unto us. If Jesus was made my righteousness, I am so fortified, so surrounded, and so protected that no being in the universe can say anything against me, because God has declared me righteous.

But He did not stop there; 2 Corinthians 5:21 says that God *"hath made him to be sin for us, who knew no sin…"* God made Jesus to become sin. Why? *"That we might be made the righteousness of God in him."* So, by the new birth, I am now the righteousness of God in Him.

I make my boast. I set up my banner. Here I raise my Ebenezer. (See 1 Samuel 7:12.) Here I sit in the presence of my enemies and eat without fear. (See Psalm 23:5.) Here I take my stand, raise my banner, and sing my songs of praise.

That old inferiority complex is gone; the old sense of unworthiness has been swallowed up in the worthiness of my Lord. The old sense of weakness is gone, and I stand complete in all His completeness.

"I have been raised with Christ."

This means that when Christ was raised from

the dead, I was raised with Him. When Christ was justified, I was justified.

When Christ was born again, I was born again. When Christ was healed of my diseases, which were laid upon Him, I was healed with His healing. When He was made strong after having borne my weaknesses, I was made strong with His strength.

His righteousness is mine; His healing is mine. His redemption, His life, and His resurrection are all mine. I am raised together with Him.

"I will reign with Jesus."

But listen! Ephesians 2:6 says that He has *"made us sit* [reign] *together in heavenly places in Christ Jesus."* What does that mean? He is seated in the highest seat of authority and the highest place of honor in the universe. I am seated with Him.

My voice grows hushed; my heart stands back in wonder and awe. I can understand how I can conquer the devil. I can understand how I can become the righteousness of God in Him. I can understand love like that, but when He says that I am seated with Him, I dare not whisper equality, although that is what it means.

Such grace I cannot understand. I was a sinner, a child of Satan. I was sin; I was unrighteous. I was all that, and more.

Now I am the righteousness of God in Him. I am united with Him. I am a part of Him. My body is a member of His body. My life is hidden with Christ in God (see Colossians 3:3); I am seated with Him. I am one with Him on the throne.

O Satan, where is thy victory? O death, where is thy clanging, hideous fear? (See 1 Corinthians 15:54–56.) My Lord, in His place, reached down and lifted me by His side onto the throne.

I reign with Christ. All things are put underneath His feet—and beneath my feet. He is head over all things, and I am in Him. As the bride is to the husband, so is the church to Christ. (See Ephesians 5:25–27.) O Bridegroom, mine! O Lord of my life!

By faith, I swing free from the bondage of age-old fear and stand complete in Him, my Lord, my own. (See Colossians 2:10.)

"I am like Christ in this world."

"As he is, so are we in this world" (1 John 4:17). I climb around this Scripture as I would around a mighty mountain peak, I gaze up into the blue sky where it pierces even to the throne of God, and I whisper through lips that can scarcely articulate, "Master, do You mean it? As You are, so are we in this world? You are holy."

"But you are holy with My holiness."

"You are the Son of God."

"But you are the sons of God. Has not the Father honored you? Has not the Father's Spirit borne witness with your spirits that you are the sons of God? (See Romans 8:16.) Come on up and sit at the table with the sons of God."

Do not live a servant's life any longer; come out of it, up into sonship privileges and a son's place in the Father's heart of love. Sit at the table and feast with Him.

"I am a victor in this world."

Victors? Oh, *"in all these things we are more than conquerors through him that loved us"* (Romans 8:37). The heart hardly dares to travel in this atmosphere; it is so new, so utterly unusual.

As He is next to the Father's heart, as He is in the Father's counsels, as He is in the Father's confidence, as He basks in the Father's love, so do we down here.

We did not know it. They told us from the pulpit, and they told us in the pews that we were poor, weak, unworthy ones, unfit and unclean. We dared not lift our faces or ever lift our eyes to look on the coveted things and the coveted treasures of sonship.

Now, with one stroke, God has wiped away the false notions, the fears of the clerics, and the creeds. We stand complete in Him in the fullness of His wonderful grace, sons and daughters of God forever done with weakness, forever done with fear, forever done with failure.

"No one can condemn me now."

We stand complete. I read again, *"It is God that justifieth. Who is he that condemneth?"* (Romans 8:33–34).

I hear condemnation on every side. I hear the jarring notes of fear. I hear the plaints, the scandals, and the recrimination as it falls from bitter lips, but He whispers into the depths of this heart of mine: "Who is he that condemns the one I have justified?"

My heart sings its solo until it finally reaches the grand chorus of the redeemed. I become a member of that redemptive choir, and I sing my part in the oratorio of grace and love and praise to my Father, who has declared me righteous in the face of all my enemies.

– 7 –
THE POWER OF AFFIRMATIONS

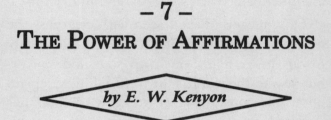

by E. W. Kenyon

I once doubted the efficacy of affirmations, but when I read in the first five books of Moses the expression "I am Jehovah" occurring more than twenty-five hundred times, then I knew the value of affirming, reiterating, and confessing the fullness of Jesus Christ and of His finished work in the presence of my weakness; in the presence of my enemies; in the presence of hell.

I would suggest that the reader constantly affirm to his own soul the great, outstanding facts of redemption. They may not mean much the first time you repeat them, but constantly reaffirm them. By and by, the Spirit will illumine them, and your soul will be flooded with light and joy.

Every time I repeat what God has said about the church, about Himself, and about me as an individual, these truths reach down deep into my inner being with strength, joy, and victory.

Only recently have I seen with clearness the infinite value of continually affirming not only to our inner man—our own soul and spirit—but also to the world. Our spiritual lives depend upon our constantly affirming what God has declared, what God is in Christ, and what we are before the Father in Christ.

The thing that made Methodism so mighty in its early days was a continual confession of the things for which John Wesley stood. When they stopped affirming, faith stopped growing, and believing or acting upon the Word became more and more difficult.

Maintain Your Testimony

I can remember when I dared not confess what God says I am. And my faith sank to the level of my confession.

If I dared not say I was the righteousness of God, Satan took advantage of my confession.

If I dared not say that my body was perfectly well and that Satan had no dominion over it, disease and pain followed my negation.

The Power of Affirmations

Since I have learned to know Christ and to know His redemptive ability, as well as to know our ability in Christ, I have been able to maintain a testimony, a confession of the completeness of the finished work of Christ, of the utter reality of the new birth.

The text of *The Power of Affirmations* is taken from "Dare You Confess That You Are What God Says You Are?" *Kenyon's Herald of Life,* July 1941, 2; "The Potency of Affirming What God Says," *Living Messages,* February 1930, 30; and "Confession," *Living Messages,* April 1930, 45, as quoted in *E. W. Kenyon and His Message of Faith: The True Story* by Joe McIntyre (Lake Mary, FL: Charisma House, 1997), 260–262.

– 8 –
THE BELIEVING HEART AND THE CONFESSING MOUTH

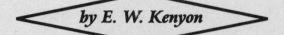

by E. W. Kenyon

Confession, or testimony, holds a larger place in the drama of redemption than the church has ever given it. When the Word tells us to *"hold fast our confession"* (Hebrews 4:14 NKJV), it means that we are to hold fast to our testimony of what God is to us, what He has done for us, what He has done in the past, and what He is doing in us now.

If the Lord heals you, you must tell it; if the Lord heals your spirit, heals your mind, heals your body, you must tell it. Go home and tell what wondrous things the Lord has wrought. If you are afraid to tell it, you will lose the blessing that belongs to you. If men can frighten you so you will not give your testimony, in a little while you will have no testimony to give. Public confession (giving your testimony) and faith are so closely related that if you lose your testimony, your faith will die out immediately. When you keep your testimony clear by continuously giving it wisely in the spirit, your faith will grow by leaps and bounds.

Boldness in Testimony

How often we sit in prayer meetings and listen to people giving what is called a testimony when they are not witnessing of Christ. They are witnessing of their own doubts and fears, or perhaps their own fancies or some hobby, rather than witnessing to the saving power of the work of Christ and the joy they have in communion and fellowship with the Father through the Spirit.

Just a word in regard to testifying—the very word *testify* gives us an inkling. We are on the witness stand and are going to say something that will glorify our Lord; we want to win the case for Him. We want the unsaved people who hear to accept Him as their Savior, and we desire that the words that we speak shall encourage weaker believers to abandon themselves more entirely to His care.

I cannot believe that we should testify because

it is our duty, but our witness should flow from hearts filled with a desire to do it because He has been so good to us.

We should not eulogize ourselves, but Him of whom we witness.

I was recently in a meeting during which the young converts testified. One after another, they rose with Bibles or New Testaments in hand and read some appropriate verse in connection with the subject on which the leader had spoken. As they wove their witness, testimony, or experience around those words, it left a very inspiring impression.

The Lord had an opportunity to work through His own Word, and the workers gave their testimony and experience and also sent forth the Word that *"shall not return unto* [Him] *void"* (Isaiah 55:11).

Developing Spiritual Power

Yes, we must witness for Him first with our lives, but we must witness for Him with our mouths, as well, for *"with the mouth confession is made unto salvation"* (Romans 10:10). Also, Jesus promised that *"whosoever...shall confess me before men, him will I confess also before my Father which is in heaven"* (Matthew 10:32).

If you want to develop the spiritual power that is within you, speak out what you have to say. It will do you more good to give a stumbling, halting testimony that is all your own than to read the most flowery thing ever written by any other man. People wish to hear real testimonies from the children of God who are on fire for Him.

People say of me that I am all right until I get to talking about my friends, and then they say I am apt to become a little enthusiastic. Get into that spirit in regard to your Father and your Savior, and you will never have any trouble giving a testimony that is your own—one that is alive and to which men and God will listen.

God wants us to witness in our daily lives with men, telling them how good and real He is to us. He desires us, through a simple confession in prayer meetings, to say we are Christians. He wishes to be highly spoken of. He wants us to magnify Him in our testimony.

The text of *The Believing Heart and the Confessing Mouth* is taken from "Testifying or Witnessing," *Reality,* December 1904, 44–45, as quoted in *E. W. Kenyon and His Message of Faith: The True Story* by Joe McIntyre (Lake Mary, FL: Charisma House, 1997), 51, 246–247.

– 9 –
THE POWER OF SPOKEN WORDS

by Don Gossett

I have put my fingers in the ears of hundreds of people who were totally deaf. Many of them didn't even have eardrums. Putting my fingers in those ears, I have spoken the words, "In the name of Jesus, I command the spirits of deafness to leave these ears. In Jesus' mighty name, I command the hearing to come in strong and normal."

The results have been miraculous. Most of the people have been completely healed so that they can hear even the faintest whispering or the ticking of a tiny wristwatch!

It overwhelms me when I consider the wonder of it! Just by speaking the words of authority, in the name of Jesus, creative miracles can take place. Physical substance is created in a moment's time as the words are spoken.

This shouldn't be as strange to us as it seems, for it was by His words that God created the world. It is by His Word that we are recreated in Christ Jesus. So we ourselves are Word products—the products of God's own wonderful, omnipotent Word. Now, when we speak His words, we are simply acting on the authority God has given us.

> *Whosoever shall say unto this mountain, Be thou removed, and be thou cast into the sea; and shall not doubt in his heart, but shall believe that those things which he saith shall come to pass; he shall have whatsoever he saith.* (Mark 11:23)

We have been instructed in God's Word to *"hold fast the profession of our faith without wavering; (for he is faithful that promised)"* (Hebrews 10:23).

As we hold fast to the confession of the Word, we are to *"affirm constantly"* (Titus 3:8) those things that God has revealed to us.

But what is confession? Is it merely when we admit to wrongdoing in our lives? In the Bible, one meaning of the word *confession* is to say or affirm what God has said in His Word about a certain thing. It is agreeing with God. It is saying the same thing the Scriptures say. To hold fast to our confession is to say what God has said over and over again until the thing desired in our hearts and promised in the Word is fully manifested. There is no such thing as possession without confession.

When we discover the rights we have in Christ, which are given throughout the Bible, we are to affirm them constantly, testify to them, and witness to these tremendous Bible facts. The apostle Paul said,

> *The communication of thy faith* [will] *become effectual by the acknowledging of every good thing which is in you in Christ Jesus.*
>
> (Philemon 1:6)

Therefore, our faith will be effective only as we confess with our mouths all the good things that are ours because we belong to Jesus.

In the book of Psalms, it says, *"Let the redeemed of the LORD say so,"* (Psalm 107:2), and again, *"Let such as love thy salvation say continually, Let God be magnified"* (Psalm 70:4).

We know that in Jesus Christ we have been given salvation, not just for our souls, but for our bodies—in our health, our finances, our peace of mind, and our freedom from bondage and fear. There are hundreds of powerful affirmations to make constantly as we speak the language of Scripture. For example:

God is who He says He is.

I am who God says I am.

God can do what He says He can do.

I can do what God says I can do.

God has what He says He has.

I have what God says I have.

Affirmations of these truths should ring from our lips constantly. We are told to hold fast to them without wavering. The penalty for wavering in our confession is that we deny ourselves God's promises and the performance of them.

> *But let him ask in faith, nothing wavering. For he that wavereth is like a wave of the sea driven with the wind and tossed. For let not that man think that he shall receive any thing of the Lord.* (James 1:6–7)

Christianity is called the Great Confession. All things in Christ—salvation, healing, and deliverance—are dependent upon our confessing the lordship of Jesus with our lips. Paul said to Timothy, *"Thou...hast professed a good profession before many witnesses"* (1 Timothy 6:12).

– 10 –
THE WORD ON OUR LIPS

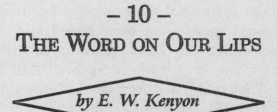

by E. W. Kenyon

Jesus wants to use our lips. Ours are the only lips He has. It is His Word on our lips that counts. He said, *"If ye abide in me, and my words abide in you…"* (John 15:7).

The Word abides on my lips and in my conversation. I preach His Word. His Word becomes mighty and living on the lips of His witnesses.

John 14:13 says, *"Whatsoever ye shall ask in my name, that will I do, that the Father may be glorified in the Son."* I saw that Scripture on Peter's lips in Acts 3:6, where he said to the lame man, *"In the name of Jesus Christ of Nazareth rise up and walk."* The words of Jesus became healing and help to that man.

I saw the Word on Paul's lips in Acts 16:18

when he said to the demon-possessed girl, *"I command thee in the name of Jesus Christ to come out of her."* She was healed.

In our ministry in Seattle, God's Word on my lips has caused the healing of hundreds of people. Cancers have been healed after four years of running sores. Discouraged, broken hearts have been made strong and filled with joy. Thousands have been saved. This ministry has been the Word of God on the lips of men and women. It is Jesus using our lips.

Revelation 12:11 says, *"And they overcame him* [Satan] *by...the word of their testimony."* The *"word"* there is *logos.* They overcame Satan by the "logos" that was in their testimony. You overcome the devil today by the "logos" in your testimony—Jesus speaking through your lips.

When I see what marvels can be done by words, I feel like saying to my lips, "You must never speak anything that does not bless and help." It is when belief is translated into language that it becomes a reality. What I think is good, but what I say is mighty.

Our words should be God-filled, logos-filled. Our words become God's words, and His words become our words, until the life that is in His Word becomes a living fact in our words, until the power and the healing virtue of His words become a reality in our words.

It is God, living in me, speaking through my lips, blessing and saving men.

– 11 –
THE POWER OF THOUGHT AND CONFESSION

by E. W. Kenyon

Criminals are not criminals by accident. They think themselves into wrongdoing. They think about crime for so long that they lose the sense of its wrongness.

Every form of wrongdoing is the product of a sequence of wrong thinking. It may take years for a man to make a murderer of himself, but he can do it. It is dreaming of doing something that, at first, shocks and horrifies, but later becomes a familiar companion, which makes the criminal.

The same thing holds true in every department of life. The great musician has to live in a mental realm of music to be able to produce it. The artist must live in the realm of great paintings and pictures. First, he dreams his picture; then, he paints it with his imagination. The great architect mentally builds his bridge years before he ever receives an order. The great novelist is first a dreamer who then puts his dream on paper. We become what we most intently think we are.

Love is largely the work of the spirit through the imagination. A man loves a woman and dreams of her until she becomes a very part of his dream life. Then, it is hard to live without her. You dream of wealth until, after a bit, your surroundings become unpleasant to you, and you will be tempted to do almost anything that will get for you the thing of which you have been dreaming.

It is imperative, if you wish to climb up into the realm called success, that you remember to master your dream life. You must absolutely govern your dreams. You must put your dream machinery to work on the right kind of fabric. If your imagination must weave, make it weave the kind of cloth that is salable.

Out of your dreams will come the masterful personality, or the weak, vacillating personality. If you want to be one of the big men or women of the future, you can do it. Your career will be molded out of the things you dream. Someone is going to be the great musician, the great statesman, the great lawyer, the great doctor, or the great architect of the future. Why should it not be you?

Almost all of the truly great men and women carved their futures out of their dream lives, even while surrounded by poverty and hardship. This is the power of your confession.

– 12 –
THE POWER OF CHRIST'S SPIRIT

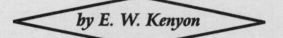

by E. W. Kenyon

Paul's personal testimony thrills me: *"For I know whom I have believed, and am persuaded that he is able to keep that which I have committed unto him against that day"* (2 Timothy 1:12).

You see, that puts the sense of mastery into a man's spirit where reason can't travel, because the way is dark. The spirit has an inward light, and that inward light is shining upon the Word that cannot fail him.

You remember what Jesus said: *"If a man love me, he will keep my words: and my Father will love him, and we will come unto him, and make our abode with him"* (John 14:23). That doesn't mean that He is going to live in your house only, but He is going to live in your heart. The Father and Jesus both are your backers, your providers, and your givers.

Jesus is made unto me wisdom from God. (See 1 Corinthians 1:30.) I have more wisdom than any enemy. I have more ability. This became true of me when I received His nature and life into my spirit. I am letting that nature dominate me.

I have love that makes me a master and a conqueror. His own love-nature has lifted me out of bitter jealousy and selfishness. He has given to me a new self—His self; a new nature—His nature; and new abilities—His own abilities. They have swallowed me up. They dominate me in Christ.

You see, a man is first beaten in his spirit, and then his rational faculties are filled with fear. It is just like an army that has lost its officers. Panic seizes them. When that inward man, the inner spirit, is in union with God, the reasoning faculties may lose their poise and be filled with panic, but the spirit is still master. Though we are filled with outward fear, there is an inward courage that drives us on to win. How many of the army boys have said to me, "Yes, I was frightened; I was filled with fear, and yet a sense of victory was in my spirit, and that was true."

The Power of Christ's Spirit

So, in all these things, we are more than conquerors. (See Romans 8:37.) We may see men defeated and failing around us, but we can't be conquered. Say it over and over again: "I cannot be conquered because God is in me, and nothing can conquer God."

– 13 –
"GOSH, SIR, ISN'T GOD WONDERFUL?"

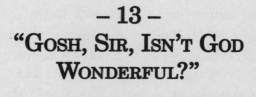

by Don Gossett

Johnny Lake was a fifteen-year-old devout Christian who lived in a town in the northern part of British Columbia. Not far from Johnny lived Dr. Riley, who had immigrated to Canada from Ireland. He was an atheist and had suffered from a painful rheumatic hip for years, but he was known throughout the area as a good doctor.

Dr. Riley took a liking to young Johnny Lake. He often took Johnny along with him on house calls. One night, they were at the home of the Owens family, where seven-year-old Cathy Owens was stricken with double pneumonia. Dr. Riley listened to the girl gasping for every breath, then finally closed his black bag.

Turning to Cathy's parents, Dr. Riley sadly announced, "I'm sorry, but Cathy won't make it through the night. I must leave now to make other calls, but I'll return later. Meanwhile, I'm leaving Johnny here to sit beside Cathy."

After Dr. Riley left the house, Johnny got down on his knees so he could speak softly into Cathy's ear: "God loves you, Cathy, and God is going to heal you." Johnny whispered, "Breathe, Cathy, breathe; O God, help Cathy to breathe."

Johnny continued, "Cathy, soon it will be spring. We'll go out on the lawn; we'll make buttercups and daisy wheels. Breathe, Cathy, breathe; O God, help Cathy to breathe.

"Then, Cathy, we'll look down a gopher hole, and maybe we'll see a gopher fairy. Breathe, Cathy, breathe; O God, help Cathy to breathe!

"Then, Cathy, we'll go to the bridge and watch the minnows in the river below as the wagons go rolling across the bridge. Breathe, Cathy, breathe! Thank You, God, You are helping Cathy to breathe!"

About two hours passed before Dr. Riley returned to the Owens' home. By this time, Johnny wasn't speaking in a whisper, but with vigor and excitement. "How long has this been going on?" Dr. Riley asked Cathy's parents.

"Ever since you left, Doctor," they replied. "There were times we thought Cathy was drawing her last breath, but now it seems she is getting stronger."

Dr. Riley took out his stethoscope, bent down, and examined Cathy. He didn't say a word, but a slow smile spread across his face. Johnny jumped up and exclaimed, "God has healed Cathy! Gosh, sir, isn't God wonderful?"

Dr. Riley responded slowly as he raised himself to his full height. Placing his hand on his own afflicted hip, he spoke the name of the One he had hated for so long, "Yes, Johnny, God is wonderful!"

At that very moment, the severe pain departed from Dr. Riley's hip.

Cathy Owens was miraculously healed of double pneumonia, Dr. Riley was totally healed of his rheumatic hip, and, best of all, Dr. Riley became a deep believer in the living Christ as his Savior and Lord—all because of the power of words spoken in faith.

Proverbs 18:21 says, *"Death and life are in the power of the tongue." The Message* translation renders it like this: *"Words kill, words give life; they're either poison or fruit—you choose."*

Johnny Lake spoke words of life and faith, words of healing and blessing. When Dr. Riley broke a lifetime of rebellion by praising God, he, too, spoke words of healing—healing for his rheumatic hip. His acknowledgment of Jesus as Lord of his life brought salvation to him.

Say it right now: "Death and life are in the power of my tongue."

God asked, "[How] *can two walk together except they be agreed?*" (Amos 3:3).

Your words are either life-producing or death-dealing, because when you choose to agree with God by speaking His Word, He walks with you in every area of your life.

Jesus is Lord of our affirmations. He is the Author and Finisher of our faith. (See Hebrews 12:2.) He is the High Priest of our confession. (See Hebrews 3:1 NKJV.)

PART II:
THE POWER IN YOUR WORDS

– 14 –
THE VALUE OF WORDS

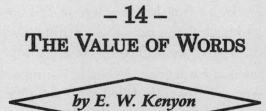

by E. W. Kenyon

Words never lie. They live on to bless or to curse. They often return to us in blessing or in judgment. How we should realize the eternal value of words!

The words of the apostle Paul are to us at times like a flame that burns; at another time, they are the healing ointment that quiets wounds and brings the heart into fellowship with heaven.

The words that Jesus spoke are still green and fresh, giving hope and joy and victory to the multitudes. The record of the things that He did still thrills us. *"The words that I speak unto you, they are spirit, and they are life,"* said the Master (John 6:63).

Now, I want you to see the effect of your words upon yourself. Your words can bring discouragement and defeat into your life.

I ask, "How are you getting along?" You answer, "Everything has gone wrong. The bottom seems to have fallen out of everything. I've lost my grip. I can't seem to complete anything."

That is a confession. What is its impact on you? You are instantly filled with self-pity and a sense of defeat. You are robbed of power, initiative, and the ability to pick up the scattered ends and bring them together again into victory. You can't seem to do it. Why? Your confession has unnerved you and wrecked you.

The same thing is true when you have trouble with your spouse or someone else, and you talk about it over and over again. Every time you do, you cry and go through the deepest agony. Had you not spoken it, you would have been much stronger.

Your words can be as poison to your own system. Your words are sometimes deadly. When you say, "I don't believe I'll ever get over this," you are taking poison. There is no antidote for it except to break the power of that kind of confession, begin to speak the right kind of words, and make the right kind of confession.

The Value of Words

If you think and speak failure, you will go down to that level. Your words will create an atmosphere that will injure and break you.

There are three classes of words. The first is neutral, colorless, empty, soulless words. These constitute the general conversation of most people. They are just empty words of the monotone. Sometimes you hear a preacher speaking in the monotone; there is no color, no soul, no power, and no life in his words—just sounds thrown out in the air.

The second class of words comprises construction words, strength-building words, healing words, and words of inspiration. These are thrilling, mighty, and dominant words, and they are pregnant with hope, love, and victory.

The third class is composed of destructive, hate-filled words full of scandal, jealousy, and deadly virus. They come from a heart full of bitterness and are sent out to wound, blight, and curse.

What a tremendous place our words hold! You see what you can do with words: you can change lives, you can bless and build and encourage others, and you can lead men to masterful achievements.

– 15 –
PUTTING YOUR BEST
INTO WORDS

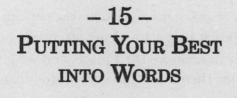

by E. W. Kenyon

Empty words hold no more interest than last year's bird's nest. When we fill our words with ourselves and we are honest, our words will be honest. Others grow to depend on them.

I know a young man whose words are filled with love and unselfishness and a desire to help people. Whenever he speaks in the company of others, they listen to him.

Nowhere else do words have as dramatic an effect as they do in a radio message. The minister who speaks over the air in a cold, dead voice will get a cold, dead response. No matter how beautiful his thoughts are or how beautifully he clothes them, if the words are not filled with love, with faith, they won't live.

Faith is built by words. Deeds have their place, but deeds are the children of words, in a large measure.

You speak, then I watch you perform. It is your speech that attracts my attention.

Your deeds have their place, and we give you credit for them, but it is your words that set us on fire.

You can fill your words with anything you wish. You can fill them with fear until the very air around you vibrates with doubt and restlessness.

You can fill your words with fear germs, and you will infect me with fear of disease and disaster. Your words can be filled with interrogation points, with a sense of lack, with hunger and want.

Or, you come to me, and your words are filled with faith. Your faith words stir me to my very depths. I wonder why I ever doubted.

Your words enwrap me within themselves. Your words are like sunlight, like coming into a warm room from a cold, frosty atmosphere outside. Your words pick up my drooping, broken spirit and fill it with confidence to go out and fight again. They are faith words, wonderful words.

Putting Your Best into Words

The reason Jesus' words had such far-reaching influence was that they were faith words. When He said to the sea, *"Peace, be still"* (Mark 4:39), the very sea grew quiet, and the winds hushed their noise to hear the words of faith from the lips of the Man.

The deaf could hear His faith words. The lame and broken could rise and walk and run because of His faith words. There was something in His words that drove disease and pain out of the body and fear out of the heart.

I can hear the disciple John say, "I used exactly the same words and that boy was not healed. Now the Master takes the words out of my lips and fills them with something, and when they are heard, the child is healed."

What did Jesus put into His words that had such healing power? He didn't just speak the words like a phonograph; He put living faith, interest, and love into his words, and therefore He received results.

The text of *Putting Your Best into Words* is taken from *Signposts on the Road to Success* by E. W. Kenyon (Kenyon's Gospel Publishing Society, 1999), 59–61.

– 16 –
ORDERING OUR CONVERSATIONS ARIGHT

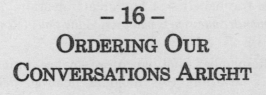

by Don Gossett

If only we would realize the power in our words, our lives would be so different. It has been said, "The pen is mightier than the sword." How much mightier the words of our pen and of our mouth when our words are the Word of God!

God declares, *"Whoso offereth praise glorifieth me: and to him that ordereth his conversation aright will I show the salvation of God"* (Psalm 50:23).

Let us consider the words we use in our conversation—and let us choose wonder-working words.

Words of Confession of God's Word

Confession always precedes possession. Dare to say exactly what God says in His Word.

Agree with God by speaking His Word in all circumstances.

When we order our words aright, God manifests the benefits of His great salvation. *"With the mouth confession is made unto salvation"* (Romans 10:10).

Remember that when we make confession unto salvation, this includes healing, deliverance, and every spiritual and physical blessing provided for us in Christ's atonement.

Words of Praise

"I will bless the LORD at all times: his praise shall continually be in my mouth" (Psalm 34:1). Resolve to be a bold "praiser." As a praiser, extol the Lord—not so much for His gifts that you have received, but to magnify the wonderful Giver for who He is.

Words of Edification and Grace

Resolve to order your conversation aright:

> *Let no corrupt communication proceed out of your mouth, but that which is good to the use of edifying, that it may minister grace unto the hearers.* (Ephesians 4:29)

Words of Health

Words have great impact on our health.

People enslaved by illness have a tendency to say, "I'm getting a cold," or "I'm coming down with the flu," or "I'm not feeling well today."

On the other hand, people who walk in divine health proclaim, "I am rarely ill because germs can't reach me," and "I refuse to give in to illness."

Faith-Filled Words

The time to speak in faith is when you are experiencing good health and feeling great. Don't wait until you are sick to begin speaking words of health and vitality over your body. Here are words to speak daily:

Thank You, Lord Jesus, that You are my Healer. Every organ, muscle, and fiber of my body functions as You intended it to. My youth is renewed like the eagle's. My life is redeemed from destruction. I have energy to accomplish what You have called me to do.

Words of Bold Authority Overcome Satan's Power

And they overcame him [Satan] *by the blood of the Lamb, and by the word of their testimony.* (Revelation 12:11)

Jesus commanded, *"Lay hands on the sick, and they shall recover"* (Mark 16:18).

You provide the hands; the Lord Jesus provides the healing! Emphasize His sure promises, for *"they are life unto those that find them, and health to all their flesh"* (Proverbs 4:22).

– 17 –
THE INFERIORITY COMPLEX

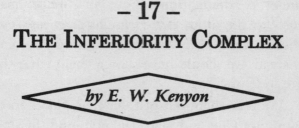

by E. W. Kenyon

The church has always taught sin-consciousness rather than righteousness-consciousness. We have been taught that we are weak, sinful, and unworthy until our prayers become, "God, oh God, have mercy upon my poor soul."

The whole thing is anti-Christ, and we did not know it; it is anti-redemption, and we did not realize that when a man becomes a child of God, he has God's nature—God's very life—in him. That nature and life give him a standing with the Father.

"There is therefore now no condemnation to them which are in Christ Jesus" (Romans 8:1). And Paul cried out, *"Who shall lay any thing to the charge of God's elect?"* (Romans 8:33). It is God who has declared you righteous and justified you.

We preachers have done a vast injury to the cause of Christ, however unwittingly. Our greatest sermons are those that put men and women under condemnation—those that make them rush to the altar, crying for forgiveness—even though they have walked with God for years. Instead, we should have shown them what they are in Christ.

We tear them out of their true places in the family of God and place them among the unregenerate. We use God's reproving message to Israel through the prophets against the church instead of lifting the church and showing believers what they are in Christ so that they can become an overcoming body. We belabor them with invective and bitter criticism.

It is like clubbing a sheep that has been kept in a desert place where there was no grass; we club it because it is poor, weak, and sickly. Let the ministers open the Word and feed believers on the food of the mighty, and they will become strong.

We have thought that the confession of our sin was a proof of our goodness, and so we have confessed our shortcomings and our failings; every testimony of ours has been of our lack, of our want, and of our weakness.

The Inferiority Complex

We have never said, *"My God shall supply all [my] need"* (Philippians 4:19) nor *"I can do all things through Christ which strengtheneth me"* (Philippians 4:13) nor *"God is the strength of my heart"* (Psalm 73:26) nor *"It is God which worketh in [me] both to will and to do of his good pleasure"* (Philippians 2:13).

If God hasn't made provision whereby we can live without condemnation, then He has failed in redemption. If the redemption does not take us out of Satan's dominion and the new birth does not take the devil nature out of us, then God has failed, and it is not our fault.

But He says, *"Therefore if any man be in Christ, he is a new creature: old things are passed away; behold, all things are become new"* (2 Corinthians 5:17). We have a new nature, we have a new relationship, we are the children of God; we have a new Father, the Father God. We stand complete in His completeness, and we are filled with His fullness; we are members of His very body.

We are the sons and daughters of God Almighty. We have been recreated by Himself, through His own Word, and we stand in His completeness.

– 18 –
SELF-DEPRECATING WORDS

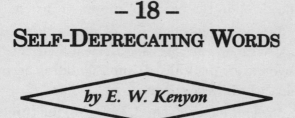

by E. W. Kenyon

There are those who always say, "Well, I have no faith. I am a doubting Thomas. I am poor and weak."

What is the effect of those words upon yourself? If you are doubting, you will doubt the more. If you are weak, the words have made you weaker. If you have been useless before, you are even more useless now because the words have made it difficult for you to be anything other than what you have said.

In the final analysis, our words are a part of ourselves; they are ourselves. If your words are full of love and peace and fidelity, they are born out of your heart life. If your words are tinged with bitter venom and sarcasm, it is because there is a vat down inside of you that is filled with that kind of material.

You create a mental condition with your words. Your words go out into the air to thrill and throb in the hearts of those that listen.

Life is largely made up of words. We make love with words. We declare war with words. Divorces are made up of words. Children become what words make them.

When I look at a child, I can feel the throb of the words that have seeped into his consciousness before he left home. The mother's words of encouragement and comfort make the child what he is.

I venture to say that the girls and boys who break down in school because of stress over study and work are the results of poor mental atmospheres in their homes. These atmospheres are word atmospheres.

Let us be careful about words. Let's put the biggest, richest things into them. Let's put big, rich words into the letters and articles that we write. Let's fill our words with wonderful love, fresh from the heart of the Father.

– 19 –
DON'T SHRINK BACK FROM BEING USED BY GOD

by Don Gossett

In 1979, the Lord of the Harvest sent me to India. This was the beginning of an ongoing ministry that has resulted in hundreds of thousands of dear people receiving Christ as their personal Savior and confessing Him as Lord of their lives. The key to this ministry of the miraculous is the power of spoken faith.

Dr. Kenyon's anointed writings motivated me to list twelve affirmations on the flyleaf of my Bible. Before each service, attended by multitudes, I confess and believe these truths. If you have a genuine hunger to be used by the Lord in effective ministry, make these dynamic affirmations yours. Speak them with confidence and be enormously blessed!

► As I use the name of Jesus according to the Word, in the power of the Spirit, I have the secret that the apostles used to shake the world. Jesus said, "You do the asking, and I will do the doing." (See John 14:14.) If I don't pray or command in His name, I don't give Him the opportunity to manifest His power. His name on my lips is the same as if Jesus were present and operating.

► If I shrink back, God has no pleasure in me. (See Hebrews 10:38.) This truth has spurred me on through many rough places. God can act through me. God has put His power in my hands and says, "Use My name, My Word, and My power—according to My will."

► I may think that the need is too great, that the sickness is unconquerable, and that my faith is too small—and all this may be true. But I have confidence in the name of Jesus, not in my own faith. In that great name, I command the sickness to go. I say, "In the name of Jesus, I command you to go." Satan dares not face a warrior who is clothed in Christ's righteousness and who knows the power of that mighty name. God's integrity, His omnipotence, and Christ's unlimited power back up my command and are all at my disposal.

Don't Shrink Back from Being Used by God

▶ I use the name of Jesus, though I may tremble when I do it. It is not I that am great, but that His name is great. I do not need to feel its power—I know it. Everything must bow to the all-conquering name of Jesus. What the rod was in the hands of Moses, Christ's name is in my mouth. It was not Moses who was great, but the power of God in the rod that was great.

▶ The only question is, *Do I understand what God means in giving me the use of His name?* To use Jesus' name does not require any unusual faith, because His name belongs to me. He has put absolutely no limitations upon the use of it. *"And whatsoever ye do in word or deed, do all in the name of the Lord Jesus, giving thanks to God and the Father by him"* (Colossians 3:17).

▶ I hurl the matchless name of Jesus against the hosts of hell, and they fly in confusion. I walk among men as a man of God. The enemy may be stubborn and resist me, but my will is set. I am going to win, and I literally charge the enemy in that all-conquering name. I refuse to give up my confession— that the name of Jesus is superior to all other names or things. *"God...hath highly exalted him,*

*and given him a name which is above every name…
of things in heaven, and things in earth, and things
under the earth"* (Philippians 2:9–10). In this
great name I command the mountain to go.
It will go. It must go!

▶ God has given me the coin of the unseen
kingdom. I use His name with a fearless
abandonment that is absolutely thrilling. I
live and walk in the realm of the supernatural. "That name has lost none of the power
of the Man who bore it."[1] The Father con-
ferred upon Him the highest name in the
universe.

▶ As I cast out devils in His name, I am amazed
at the strange reverence that comes over me
as I exercise—by a simple command—this
marvelous power, witnessing many startling
results. I cannot conceive how successful
work can be done today, or how I could be
in a place of continual victory over the spirits of darkness, without the name of Jesus of
Nazareth, the Son of God.

▶ "The more quickly I recognize that the very
air about us is filled with hostile forces, who
are attempting to destroy our fellowship
with the Father, and to deprive us of our

usefulness in the service of the Master, the better it will be for [me]."[2] All power is in the name of the risen Christ Jesus who is seated at the Father's right hand in the heavens.

▶ I cannot use the name of Jesus effectively while out of fellowship with God. It is vitally important that I stay in fullest fellowship at every moment. If I lose my spiritual initiative, I lose something that will drive me through the hard places.

▶ I cannot afford to take a negative attitude toward the Word. If I do, my holy fearlessness will be lost, and my heart will not say, *"I can do all things through Christ which strengtheneth me"* (Philippians 4:13). And when my spiritual initiative is low, I will not be able to say, "Greater is He that is in me than the forces that surround me." (See 1 John 4:4.) If my heart loses its boldness and fearlessness in acting on the Word, I will be in danger.

▶ I will take my permanent place and abide where I may enjoy the fullness of His mighty power. My confession must absolutely agree with the Word. When I have prayed or commanded in Jesus' name, I hold fast to my confession. It is easy to destroy the effect of my prayer by a negative confession. I will continue to confess that when I speak the name of Jesus it is the same as if Jesus were speaking.

Such as I have give I thee: In the name of Jesus Christ of Nazareth rise up and walk.

(Acts 3:6)

[1] Kenyon, E. W., *The Wonderful Name of Jesus.* (Kenyon's Gospel Publishing Society, 1998), 11.

[2] Ibid., 19.

of the Troubled Mind

If thou wilt not observe to do all the words of this law... the Lord will make thy plagues wonderful...
(Deuteronomy 28:58-59).

– 20 –
LOOSE TALKING

by E. W. Kenyon

Careless speech is a vicious habit. When one realizes that his words are the coin of his kingdom and that his words can be either a cursing influence or a blessing, he will learn to value the gift of speech.

Control your tongue, or it will control you. You will often hear men say, "I speak my mind." That is well if you have a good mind, but if your mind is poisoned, it is not good. An idle word spoken aloud may fall into the soil of someone's heart and poison his entire life.

What a blessing good conversation is and what a curse its opposite!

Make your tongue always a blessing, never a curse. A person is judged by his speech. Your words make you either a blessing or a curse. Your words may carry a fortune in them. Learn to be master of your conversation.

The text of *Loose Talking* is taken from *Signposts on the Road to Success* by E. W. Kenyon (Kenyon's Gospel Publishing Society, 1999), 32.

– 21 –
"DON'T BREAK ME WITH WORDS!"

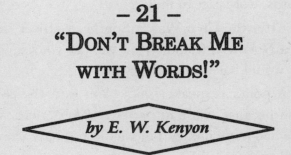

by E. W. Kenyon

Don't break me with words!" This was Job's cry to his friends. (See Job 19:2.) They came as comforters. They stayed as tormentors.

Words heal and words break; words destroy and words make life as we find it today. Words heal us and words make us ill. Words bless us and words curse us. The words I just heard will linger throughout the day.

How little a woman realizes that a biting, stinging word in the morning will rob her husband of efficiency through an entire day. A loving, tender, beautiful word—a little prayer word—will fill him with music that will lead him on to victory. We need the music of faith that only our loved ones can give to us.

How little we have appreciated the tremendous power of words—written words, spoken words, words set to music.

After the Civil War, a Southern officer said to a Northern friend, "Had we had your songs, we would have conquered you."

A political speaker said, "You won the election because you had better speakers than we. We had more money, but we did not have words well spoken."

You see, men and women, a study in words is one of the most valuable assets in life. Learn how to make words work for you. Learn how to make words burn. Learn to fill words with power that cannot be resisted.

During World War II, Mussolini held Italy in his hand by the power of his words. Austria was conquered by Hitler with words—no powder, no poison gas, no bayonets—just words.

How we wait for a message made up of words. The secret of advancement in life lies in the ability to say the right kind of words. My ministry over the radio is a ministry of words. I fill them with love; I ask God to fill them with Himself, and so I send them out to bless and cheer.

Mothers, your home atmosphere is a product of words. Your son or daughter might have failed because wrong words were spoken and right words were not spoken.

Why is it that some children grow up so clean and strong, fight their way through college, and go out in life's fight and win? It is because the right kind of words were spoken in the home. Words make a girl love education. Words bring a boy to church or keep him away.

Think of something of infinite importance and learn to choose the right words to express it. Then, send the words out with pen or tongue. The way you say it has tremendous weight.

Every public speaker should make a study of words, the kind of words that count. Then, before he leaves his study, he should so charge his mind with God and God's ability that when he stands before the people, that ability will fill his words until the people are thrilled.

He should make the delivery of words a study, an art. He should fill all his words with kindness, with love.

Try out words in your own home to see how

they work. Fill your lips with lovely words, beautiful words, until men will love to meet you and long to hear you speak. Remember, words are apples of gold in settings of silver. (See Proverbs 25:11.)

The text of *Don't Break Me with Words!* is taken from *Signposts on the Road to Success* by E. W. Kenyon (Kenyon's Gospel Publishing Society, 1999), 64–66.

– 22 –
WORDS CAN WORK BLUNDERS

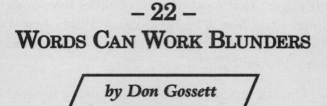

by Don Gossett

Words can work wonders, but they can also work blunders! Do you realize that multitudes of people fail in life because they speak failure? They fear failure and allow their fear to overcome their faith.

What you say locates you. You will not—you cannot—rise above your own words. If you speak defeat, failure, anxiety, sickness, and unbelief, you will live on that level. Neither you nor anyone else, no matter how clever, will ever live above the standard of their conversation. This spiritual principle is unalterable.

If your conversation is foolish, trifling, impractical, or disorganized, your life invariably will be the same way. With your words, you constantly paint a public picture of your inner self.

Jesus said, *"Out of the abundance of the heart the mouth speaketh"* (Matthew 12:34).

If you think back on your life, you will probably agree that most of your troubles have been tongue troubles. The Bible says, *"Whoso keepeth his mouth and his tongue keepeth his soul from troubles"* (Proverbs 21:23).

Oh, the trouble caused by an unruly tongue! Words spoken in the heat of the moment—words of anger, words of harshness, words of retaliation, words of bitterness, words of unkindness—these words produce trouble for us. Beloved, let's make this our prayer right now:

> *Let the words of my mouth, and the meditation of my heart, be acceptable in thy sight, O LORD, my strength, and my redeemer.*
>
> (Psalm 19:14)

Here's another good Bible prayer: *"Set a watch, O LORD, before my mouth; keep the door of my lips"* (Psalm 141:3).

It's really important that we let God help us overcome our unruly speech habits, for our words can work blunders and get us into trouble. A negative confession can produce negative results. The Bible warns, *"Thou art snared with the words of thy mouth, thou art taken with the words of thy mouth"* (Proverbs 6:2).

Confession is made with the mouth, not only for the good things God has promised us, but also for sickness, defeat, bondage, lack, and failure.

Refuse to have a bad confession. Refuse to have a negative confession. Repudiate a dual confession when you are saying at one moment, *"with his stripes we are healed"* (Isaiah 53:5) and at the next moment, "But the pain is still there."

Go to higher level of living in the kingdom of God. Believe that you are who God says you are. Think that way. Talk that way. Act that way. Train yourself to live on the level of what is written about you in God's Word.

Do not permit your thoughts, your words, or your actions to contradict what God says about you.

Although you may not master positive confession in a day or even a week, you will learn it as you continue to walk in it faithfully. Because He has said it, we may boldly say the same thing!

– 23 –
WITH THE HEART, MAN BELIEVETH UNTO RIGHTEOUSNESS

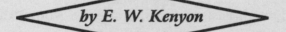

by E. W. Kenyon

If thou shalt confess with thy mouth the Lord Jesus, and shalt believe in thine heart that God hath raised him from the dead, thou shalt be saved.
—Romans 10:9

When we believe in the heart, it is because the heart has been adjusted to the Father. Man is in the same class with God. God is a spirit. Man is a spirit. When man, the spirit, is rightly adjusted with the Father and begins to feed on the Word, and his mind becomes fruitful and renewed, then faith becomes a normal, natural thing.

When I believe with my heart, that means that my spirit is in agreement with the Word. Faith is developed just as love is developed. Love is developed by exercising it. The more I love, the more I am capable of loving. Faith is developed by acting on the Word of God. Every time I act on the Word, my faith becomes stronger.

For instance, if I am sick in my body, I see that "by His stripes I am healed." (See Isaiah 53:5.) I act on the Word. The Word says God laid my disease on Jesus. I take the ground that if Jesus bore my disease, I need not bear it. I act on the Word. I get up and go about my work.

I feel physical weakness in my body. I find my mind does not grasp things as it should. Yet I declare that my mind shall become the mind of Christ, that my will shall become the will of Christ, that the life of God shall so fill my spirit that the life, love, and nature of the Father will take me over until it is no longer I who lives, but the God of life who dominates and lives in me.

We feed our love nature with words. We either write love words to the object of our love or we speak love words. Words are a necessity. Every time we speak words of love, love develops and grows stronger. Love never breaks its boundaries until we have confessed our love first to ourselves, then to the object of our affection. When we confess love, it passes out of our control and becomes the property of another. Every time we say, "Master, I love You," or we say before the world, "I love my Lord," we are confessing love. Every time we act and do love, love grows.

The same thing is true with righteousness. Righteousness is not a mental or physical thing. It is a spiritual thing. Our righteousness is the righteousness of our spirits. I act out righteousness—that is, I do the things that a righteous one would do. What are those things? A righteous one is fearless in the presence of the Father because righteousness means the ability to stand in His presence fearlessly, to stand in the presence of Satan and death without fear or condemnation. It means the ability to stand in the Father's presence as though sin and weakness and failure have never been.

When I practice righteousness, I am practicing something on my own spirit nature. I go out and dare to pray with the sick, I dare to talk the Jesus kind of talk and dare to live the Jesus kind of life. That is righteousness in life, in action, and in conduct.

Love grows with confession. Faith grows with confession. Righteousness-consciousness grows with confession. Every time I confess my righteousness in Christ, or God's righteousness in me, I begin to develop and grow. Every time I confess my faith, my faith grows. If one never confesses, one never grows. Your growth is measured by your confession. Just as we feed love with words, we feed faith with words—our words and God's Word. If I talk unbelief and weakness and failure, my spirit will go down to the level of my words. My faith will grow weak and feeble. My righteousness will be of no effect. The Word of God loses its power in me.

Then, I talk God talk, faith talk, righteousness talk. I talk the Word of God. I confess what I am in Christ and what God says I am. I talk the big talk of the realm of the Spirit, and unconsciously I move into the fullness of His strength.

I say, "Greater is He that is in me than the forces that are opposed to me." (See 1 John 4:4.) I confess that God is my righteousness now and that I have a right to be in His presence. I make my petitions and my appeals to Him in prayer. Being the righteousness of God, I can lay hands on the sick and they must recover. God being my righteousness and the strength of my life, I can use the name of Jesus effectively.

This is believing in the heart:

> *That if thou shalt confess with thy mouth the Lord Jesus, and shalt believe in thine heart that God hath raised him from the dead, thou shalt be saved. For with the heart man believeth unto righteousness; and with the mouth confession is made unto salvation.* (Romans 10:9–10)

There can be no belief in the heart until there is confession with the lips.

The measure of my faith will be the measure of my confession. Holding fast to our confession is one of the necessities of our daily lives. Jesus maintained His confession even before Pontius Pilate. He made His confession on the cross. He said, *"Father, forgive them; for they know not what they do"* (Luke 23:34). What a confession that was! It took Him out of the sense realm and into the realm of the spirit.

I hold fast to my confession that God is my

Father, and that He is greater than all; that my God does supply my every need. (See Philippians 4:19.) I hold fast to that confession with joy. I hold fast to that confession even in the presence of lack, knowing that my need cannot exist. I know that my need is going to be swallowed up in my confession of the promises of God.

– 24 –
JUST A WORD OF WARNING

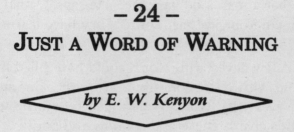

by E. W. Kenyon

Children's lives are largely made up of words—the words of their parents and those whom they love and admire. A mother can fill her son's heart with zeal for an education and for a position in life, or she can, with words, destroy the finest spirit that was ever given to a home.

A wife little appreciates the power of her words on her husband's life. If he loses his job, she could scold him and tell him that he is no good. He was whipped before he came home, but he would then be doubly whipped.

Instead, she must put her arms around him and say, "That's all right, dear. You will get a better position. You are worthy of a better job, anyway."

He goes out the next morning thrilled by

the touch of her lips; her words have filled him with courage and confidence. He leaves her heart filled with joy and gladness, and she says, "What a man God gave me." He says, "What a woman You gave me, Lord." They have learned the secret of words.

A few devastating words could have filled his mind with confusion, his heart with pain, and his eyes with tears. Words give heartache, or words give strength and comfort and faith.

Let's be careful of the words we use. Don't tell that story you heard the other day about this man or that woman. Don't let any other ears be poisoned as your ears have been poisoned with it.

Never repeat scandal. Never repeat talk of calamity. Let others do the talking about that. You keep your lips for beautiful things, helpful things, comforting things. That is your job.

The text of *Just a Word of Warning* is taken from *Signposts on the Road to Success* by E. W. Kenyon (Kenyon's Gospel Publishing Society, 1999), 38–39.

– 25 –
WAILING AND FAILING GO HAND IN HAND

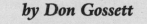

by Don Gossett

Whoso keepeth his mouth and his tongue keepeth his soul from troubles.
—Proverbs 21:23

Thou art snared with the words of thy mouth, thou art taken [captive] *with the words of thy mouth.*
—Proverbs 6:2

Jesus promised us a saved, healed life; a Spirit-filled life. Here in this verse from Proverbs 21, He promises to rescue our souls from every trouble—*"all things work together for good to them that love God"* (Romans 8:28)—if we "keep" our mouths and our tongues.

Thousands of Christians wonder, *Why is my life seemingly loaded with trouble and heartache? Why does my life have more bad than good? Why am I defeated, sick, and miserable so much of the time? Why am I beaten down and feeling hopeless?*

You may think, *I'm a believer. But why the misery? Why am I unhappy?*

The answer is that, with your own words, you have opened the door to Satan. When you speak death-dealing words, you give Satan permission to come into your life, into your affairs.

Just what are wrong words? Which words give Satan access to your life? Here are some classic examples:

- ▶ "I'll always be in debt."
- ▶ "I think I'm coming down with something."
- ▶ "It looks like we won't be able to pay our bills this month."
- ▶ "Satan is on me all the time. I just can't defeat him."
- ▶ "Well, if it's bad, it will happen to me."
- ▶ "I just know we'll have an accident."
- ▶ "I guess we will have to give up the idea of ever having a home of our own."
- ▶ "It seems like bad things always happen to us."

▶ "I am afraid I'm stuck in this situation."

▶ "We'll just have to put up with this."

▶ "These kids will never make it at the rate they are going."

▶ "I guess we won't get a vacation this year."

▶ "My folks always had poor health, so I probably will, too."

▶ "My marriage doesn't look like it's going to make it."

▶ "I just don't love my spouse anymore."

▶ "The children don't love me. They won't obey me."

▶ "It just seems we will never get anywhere."

▶ "This family is going to the dogs."

▶ "My family just doesn't want God."

When Jesus said in Mark 11:23, "[You] *shall have whatsoever* [you] *saith,*" He was describing a powerful law of faith that works for good or bad, for sickness or health, for supply or lack, for defeat or victory. When you speak words like the ones listed above, you give place to Satan.

Satan will deliver to you what you have said. He seems to say, in his destructive way, "You've declared these things, and you can trust me to do them. I surely won't fail you."

Unless you speak in faith, your enemy will see to it that you reach the level of your own words.

– 26 –
THE "NOW" JESUS

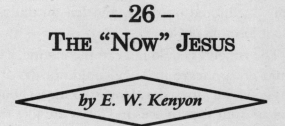

by E. W. Kenyon

Jesus Christ the same yesterday,
and to day, and for ever.
—Hebrews 13:8

The word "Jehovah" has three tenses: past, present, and future. There are also three tenses in redemption: what He did and was, what He is and what He is doing, and what He will be and do. What He was, He is. What He is now, He will be tomorrow.

The most unique feature of this is that the Word He spoke in the past is now. His Word is living now. It is authoritative now. It has the power to save now. It has the power to heal now.

Exodus 16:18–20 tells the story of the Israelites receiving manna in the desert. The manna had to be gathered every morning. If any was left over until the next day, it became sour, unfit to eat. So it is with the Word. It must be studied daily, meditated on daily, and fed on daily, or else it loses its power.

The Israelites could not can the manna. They could not preserve it. They could not dry it. It was good only for a day. How striking a thought that is! Your experiences in Christ are like that. The experience of yesterday is of no value now. Many of us have tried to preserve our experiences. It can't be done. It is the "now" Jesus. What Jesus said must always be experienced anew, here in the "now." It is what He is doing now, what He is now.

When He said, "*Whatsoever ye shall ask the Father in my name, he will give it you*" (John 16:23), that truth was to last until He came back again. When He said, "*In my name…they shall lay hands on the sick, and they shall recover*" (Mark 16:17–18), that promise was to last until He came back again. The Word is as fresh as though it had been spoken yesterday. When He said, "*If two of you shall agree on earth as touching any thing that they shall ask, it shall be done for them*" (Matthew 18:19), that truth is just as new and fresh as though He had uttered it this morning. "*If ye abide in me, and my words abide in you, ye shall ask what ye will, and it shall be done unto you"* (John 15:7) is just as fresh as though He had said it an hour ago.

No Word from God ever grows old. It has perennial freshness. It renews itself continually.

– 27 –
BE HUMBLE OR YOU WILL TUMBLE

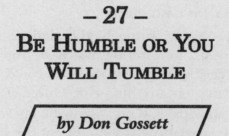

by Don Gossett

Faith is a fruit of humility. *"God resisteth the proud, but giveth grace unto the humble"* (James 4:6). One of the most challenging yet triumphant experiences of my life involved the relationship between true humility and the confession of God's Word for healing.

In 1976, I was oppressed with very painful headaches from the top of my head to the back of my neck. The pain was nearly more than I could stand. I had received miraculous healings from both an enlarged heart and a cancerous growth as a result of boldly speaking God's Word, but though I spoke the healing Word repeatedly, my headaches were unrelenting. Finally, I visited my family physician. He assured me that he could give me a prescription that would take care of the headaches. He was sincerely mistaken.

Weeks dragged by, and the headaches remained my primary concern. Then, we traveled overseas for ministry.

I was going through the daily speaking assignments, ministering mostly by rote. With the intense pain in my head, I could hardly concentrate on anything else. One day, a high school principal and his wife made my wife and me their special guests for a tour of the area and a nice lunch. However, the pain in my head was increasing to such a level that I could barely endure the day's activities.

After preaching that night, depression and self-pity hit me like a blast of dynamite. I tumbled into bed with these morbid words: "I don't want to live another day. I hope I will die in my sleep tonight. These pains are so miserable, I just can't stand them." My wife was not impressed by my negativity.

After a fitful night, I awakened to discover my prayer had not been answered: I was still alive. I announced to my wife that I was going to the prayer closet in our friend's home, and I wasn't going to come out until I heard from the Lord about my wretched condition. When

Be Humble or You Will Tumble

I arrived at the prayer closet, I locked the door from the inside so no one could disturb me.

The words of Psalm 34:6 came forcibly to me: *"This poor man cried, and the LORD heard him, and saved him out of all his troubles."*

I felt as if I was that desperate man as I stretched myself out on the carpet of that room. I cried out with tears, "Lord, why has my healing not been manifested? I have confessed Your healing Word, I have praised Your name, and I have searched my heart. I have prayed and fasted. Why have I not received my healing?"

The Holy Spirit responded to my request for Him to search my heart and reveal the hindrance to my healing. He made known to me that I had a spirit of pride that was preventing the manifestation of healing for my excruciating headaches.

Quickly the Scriptures began to rise up in my spirit:

> *Be clothed with humility: for God resisteth the proud, and giveth grace to the humble. Humble yourselves therefore under the mighty hand of God, that He may exalt you in due time.*
> (1 Peter 5:5–6)

> [Serve] *the Lord with all humility.*
> (Acts 20:19)

He hath showed thee, O man, what is good; and what doth the LORD require of thee, but to do justly, and to love mercy, and to walk humbly with thy God? (Micah 6:8)

The Holy Spirit spoke these words to my spirit: "Any time you are proud, the Lord must resist you. If your prayers are not answered, if your finances are not being provided, if you are not receiving your healing, you must examine your heart to see if you are permitting pride to prevent your request."

A High Price for Low Living

Now, if you had asked me if I thought I was bound by an attitude of pride, I would have said, "No."

The Lord showed me that it was not so much an attitude of arrogance or egotism that I had. Rather, it was an attitude of self-sufficiency. My spirit was not one of dependence on Him.

When I realized that this attitude of pride was keeping God from healing me of the headaches, I cried out, "Lord, what a high price for low living! Forgive me, Lord, for having such a wrong spirit. Never again do I want to possess this attitude of pride. Cleanse me, Lord, by Your precious blood."

God forgave me and cleansed me from that ugly spirit of pride.

For the next forty-five minutes, I basked in His presence, praising the Lord and confessing His healing Word.

As I continued to speak the Word, I looked up and saw a man standing there. I quickly looked to see if the door was still locked. It was.

The stranger moved slowly toward me as I lay on the floor. He reached down and laid his hand on my head. The sensation of his touch was like warm, penetrating oil flowing into my head. All of the pain instantly left! The man stepped back, keeping his gaze on me.

I wanted this stranger to identify himself, so I asked him, "Sir, are you the apostle Paul?" I have no explanation for why I asked that question. I just knew I was a part of something tremendously supernatural.

The man replied, "I am an angel of the Lord sent to minister to you who are an heir of salvation." (That is exactly what Hebrews 1:14 declares.) After he spoke those words, the angel vanished from my sight. I never saw him again.

I sat there simply amazed that an angel of the Lord had visited me. I was healed, praise God!

That day, a new "Power Poem" was born into my spirit: "Be humble or you will tumble!"

Indeed, faith is a fruit of true humility. My confession of the healing Scriptures did not minister healing until I humbled my heart and dealt with my attitude of pride.

The story I've just told you occurred in February 1976. More than thirty years have passed since that wonderful miracle, and it is still one of the sweetest supernatural happenings of my entire life.

Equally important is this awesome fact: I have never had a headache since that long-ago day on a faraway island!

Yes, there was a satanic trap set for me the day I arrived back home, but I resisted the lying vanities that the enemy tried to push on me. Boldly I declared, "Listen, Devil, I was healed by the bleeding stripes of Jesus my Lord. You are a wicked thief who is trying to steal my healing. I refuse to be your dumping ground any longer. Be gone, Devil, in the mighty name of Jesus!"

I don't expect to have a headache ever again. Jesus dispatched His holy angel to minister that deliverance for me.

Oh, for a thousand tongues to sing my dear Savior's praise for this mighty deliverance!

"Did You Really See an Angel?"

One Sunday morning, when I was in Cairns, Queensland, Australia, ministering at an Assemblies of God church, I shared this account of the visitation of the angel of the Lord and the wondrous healing I received.

After the service, a lady named Mrs. Clarke approached me with her fifteen-year-old daughter, Cathy. "Mr. Gossett," the mother said, "my daughter has a question she wants to ask you."

I turned to the daughter, who asked, "Did you really see an angel?"

"Yes, I did, Cathy."

She gazed at me a few moments, then added, "Really?" Again, I assured her that what I had shared about the visit of the angel was completely true.

Then, I said to her, "Cathy, I have a question I would like to ask, a question far more important than the one you asked me. Have you received Jesus Christ as your personal Savior and Lord?"

She replied, "No, I haven't."

"Then, Cathy, I want to ask you another

question: Would you like to accept the Lord today, right here and now?"

Without a moment's hesitation, Cathy answered, "Yes, Mr. Gossett, I would like to do that right now." I had the joy of leading her to Jesus that Sunday morning.

She was fascinated by my testimony of being visited by an angel. My answers to her questions satisfied her. Most important, she walked away from that church a born-again child of God. That is really the most important matter!

PART III:
THE FRUITS OF SPOKEN FAITH

– 28 –
BOLDLY SAY WHAT GOD SAYS

by Don Gossett

For he hath said, I will never leave thee,
nor forsake thee. So that we may boldly say,
The Lord is my helper, and I will not fear
what man shall do unto me.
—Hebrews 13:5–6

Make God's Word the standard for your life. Train yourself to say what He says. Bring your lips under subjection. Think before you speak. Say what God says! Don't contradict Him and His Word. God is in His Word. When you confess it, He performs it! Sooner than you can imagine, a revolution will take place in your life.

When you do these things, you will find that you are truly living the bold, abundant life set forth in God's Word. I know this for certain because it has happened innumerable times in my own life and ministry.

I am blessed over and over as I remember how God provided for us during our first mission to Africa years ago. We were down to the last day before leaving that February, but we were still seventeen hundred dollars short of the necessary funds for the mission.

No matter what avenue I had pursued in obtaining the money, none had been successful. But I knew this was a time to hold my heart steady in the expectation that God Himself would minister to our need.

I quietly reaffirmed again and again, both in my heart and with my mouth, what the Word promised: *"My God shall supply all your need according to his riches in glory by Christ Jesus"* (Philippians 4:19).

When I arrived at my office that last morning, I called all our staff together. We decided we would walk with God by agreeing with God—just as I had boldly preached to thousands of others to do.

We presented our need for seventeen hundred dollars to our heavenly Father. Then, we lifted up our hands and praised the Lord in advance for His supply. We confessed the Word together for a time before returning to the normal duties of the day. We were not trying to manipulate God, nor even to "impress" Him with our earnestness in seeking His help. We were simply requesting provision from our faithful God.

While I was gone from the office, a man from Vancouver named Peter Dyck called and told my wife, "The Lord has spoken to me by His sweet inner voice, 'Give Don Gossett seventeen hundred dollars.' I don't have that much money in my bank account, but I made a loan on my credit card to secure the cash. If Brother Don can meet me on my way to work this afternoon, I will have the seventeen hundred dollars to give him."

This was one of the most miraculous divine interventions we had experienced up to that time. The Lord spoke the exact amount we needed, and the man heard His voice and obeyed Him!

I never cease to marvel at those dear people who can hear the voice of the Lord and obey Him. During a meeting that I held at a Baptist church in Duanesberg, New York, a man named Sam Sumner stood and shared the following testimony.

After I was baptized in the Holy Spirit several years ago, I was walking in a wondrous time of Spirit-led events that were beautiful. Then, one day, the Lord said to me, "I want you to send Don Gossett three hundred dollars."

I replied, "All right, Lord, I will. But I don't know who Don Gossett is, where he lives, or just how I could send him three hundred dollars."

I more or less forgot about that word until a few weeks passed. Then the Lord spoke rather firmly, "When are you going to send Don Gossett the three hundred dollars I told you to send him?"

I was a little upset about this reminder. After all, I didn't even know who Don Gossett was, or how to send him the money. I walked out to my car complaining, "Lord, You have got to let me know how I can do this!"

I drove out on the New York Thruway and turned on the radio. I was just surfing the dial when I heard these words: "You can write to Don Gossett, Box 2, Blaine, Washington, 98231." Praise God, it was like a voice from heaven!

It is quite remarkable how the Lord can speak with His inner voice and how the hearts of sincere people can hear Him and have the grace to obey lovingly.

Through a lifetime of trusting God for many things, I have learned that God desires us to speak in faith. God's responses are normally preceded by our faith words. The Lord says, *"To him that ordereth his conversation aright will I show the salvation of God"* (Psalm 50:23).

We are not mere robots without the ability to choose the words we speak. Rather, we order our conversation rightly or wrongly. God gives guidance to our conversation and motivates our words, but the choice to order our conversation is still ours. God says, "If you choose to order your conversation aright, I will show you My salvation." By this, He means salvation in every area of our lives.

Healed by Jesus of Nazareth...in Nazareth

Several years ago, I led a group of Christians to Israel. As we left Jerusalem early one morning, I was battling an intense fever, which meant there was infection raging inside me. I felt miserable as we continued our sightseeing through Israel. It was quite a battle for me.

I knew I shouldn't talk about it with my

friends, for I would certainly get their sympathy and pity and then begin to feel sorry for myself. None of those factors would help when what I needed was healing from God. I continued to maintain my quiet confession of His Word.

As I disciplined my heart and lips to speak, "Thank You, Jesus, by Your stripes I am healed" (see 1 Peter 2:24), the Lord was gracious to manifest a beautiful healing for me in the city of Nazareth, the hometown of our Lord Jesus Christ.

I immediately conducted a healing service right there on the streets of Nazareth. I announced to my group of thirty-five companions, "Most of last night and all day, I have battled a raging fever. I took a brief nap here on the bus. When I awoke, I was perspiring profusely. The fever has broken! Jesus of Nazareth has healed me right here in Nazareth!"

They all rejoiced with me. Then, I ministered to those who needed healing, and His power and love were manifested.

I would like to say to you reading this book that right now, you can begin to speak the Word and Jesus of Nazareth will be your Healer, whether you live in Canada, the United States, England, Barbados, India, or some other place.

Simply hold fast to your confession, saying, "By His stripes I am healed."

"As thy days, so shall thy strength be" (Deuteronomy 33:25). It is essential that you take the Lord's strength daily. We all know our weaknesses in life—whether spiritual, physical, or mental. Sometimes our weaknesses are in our conversations, bad habits, overindulgence in eating, watching too much television, or being consumed with unclean sexual desires and thoughts.

We have victory over those weaknesses because the Lord knows how to minister strength. Let's confess His Word: *"The LORD is the strength of my life"* (Psalm 27:1) and *"Let the weak say, I am strong"* (Joel 3:10).

Say it over and over: "In Jesus, I am strong! I am strong!" If that seems like a contradiction to your natural thinking, consider that you are moving to a higher level of life where God's Word prevails, not your negative feelings and thoughts.

The Christian life is made up of a series of adversities and problems, which God always gives us the grace to overcome. That's why God calls us "overcomers," not "those going under."

Financial Mountains

Verily I say unto you, That whosoever shall say unto this mountain, Be thou removed, and be thou cast into the sea; and shall not doubt in his heart, but shall believe that those things which he saith shall come to pass; he shall have whatsoever he saith. (Mark 11:23)

Notice that Jesus did not say, "He shall have whatsoever he thinketh." Positive thinking is powerful, but it's not "he shall have whatsoever he thinketh," rather, *"he shall have whatsoever he saith."*

Ever since the Holy Spirit taught me the enormous importance of "speaking to mountains," my finances have been literally transformed. I would like to share two of my more recent experiences. The first story involves God's provision through the help of a stranger.

Because my wife, Debra, and I are called to preach to the nations, we travel more than one hundred thousand miles every year. We have always spoken in faith for the money necessary to purchase our many airline fares, and, in 1997, the Lord responded to our spoken faith by touching the heart of one of His choice saints. For years, this lady had listened to my daily radio broadcasts, and she had often heard our reports of traveling to India, Africa, and other nations.

God Himself dropped into her heart a burden to provide complimentary tickets for our ministry. This lady had worked for one of the largest airlines in the world for more than twenty years. Through her connection with the airline, she was able to secure tickets called "Companion Passes," which she gave to us.

Almost reluctantly, we approached the airline counter with those passes in hand, and I simply told the agent that we wanted to go to Hong Kong, then on to Delhi, India. The agent promptly issued our boarding passes, and we were on our way. And not just in ordinary economy seating—we were assigned seats in business class! I was caught up with a sense of wonder.

I thought, *Not only do we have these expensive business-class seats, but the price is so right—free! Praise the Lord!*

Since 1997, we have taken dozens of these wonderful flights. Singapore. Tokyo. Paris. Frankfurt. Delhi. Hong Kong. Milan. Sydney. Melbourne. Had we paid for these flights, the cost would have been tens of thousands of dollars.

The second story is about God's provision of a car.

Before my dear first wife, Joyce, received her call to heaven, she helped me to buy a new car. That was in April 1989. For ten years, I delighted in driving that car, adding many thousands of miles each year.

As the car slowly began to wear out, my children would often say to me, "Dad, it's time for you to buy a new car."

I always responded to them by simply saying, "No, since 1950, I've signed notes and gone into debt for many different vehicles. Not again! This time, I'm going to speak the Word of the Lord for the provision of new transportation."

Debra and I continued to speak for this provision. Then, on March 17, 1999, I received a phone call from a Christian brother.

"Don, I want you and Debra to see me at my office today. Can you come?"

"Yes," I responded. "We will be there."

Upon our arrival at the man's office, he invited us to go for a ride in his vehicle. After a few blocks, he asked me to drive the vehicle. Then, later, he suggested that Debra drive. When we returned to his office, he asked us, "How do you like the vehicle?" We assured him it was very nice indeed.

Astonishingly, the man replied, "Since you like it, it's yours! Come back tomorrow, and we'll have the paperwork done, and you can take the car."

Again, this was so completely in the realm of the supernatural that we were beside ourselves with joy and delight.

You see, this was not just an ordinary vehicle. It was a 1998 Range Rover, the top of the line in the Land Rover family. We were informed it was the official vehicle of the royal family in England, where the car is made. When we saw a video describing the unique features of this Range Rover, we were once more walking on fleecy clouds of spiritual ecstasy.

Since March 1999, Debra and I have enjoyed driving this car immensely! Again, it was the Lord's provision in response to our belief-filled spoken faith. Only God could have supernaturally directed this man to be His instrument of supply. And that man could hear the voice of the Lord and obey!

"He shall have whatsoever he saith" (Mark 11:23). Who said those words? Our Master, the Lord Jesus Christ!

Did He really mean it? Yes!

Does it include finances? Most assuredly!

These two remarkable provisions have been the "icing on the cake" during our many years of speaking the Word for finances.

Do you need a job, or perhaps just a better job? Do you need a good car? Money to roof your home? Do you need new furniture to replace the worn-out items in your home? Money for dental bills? Funds for your children's education? Money for airline tickets?

Whether your area of need is financial, spiritual, or physical, this is my challenge to you:

- ► Don't talk sickness; rather, speak the healing Word.

- ► Don't talk weakness; rather, affirm that the Lord is the strength of your life.

- ► Don't talk defeat; rather, shout your victory in Jesus.

- ► Don't talk lack; rather, confess His provision for your every need.

- ► Don't talk bondage; rather, confess His freedom.

– 29 –
WE HAVE VICTORY IN JESUS' NAME

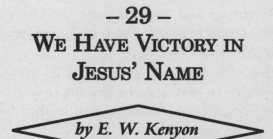

by E. W. Kenyon

The night that caused me to write the song "We Have Victory in Jesus' Name" was a fearful night. It had stormed all day. The wind had whipped into a fury, and the snow had piled up in great drifts. It stormed as only it can storm on that fearful eastern coast of the United States.

The crowd had come. Conviction was so great that it seemed like nothing could keep the folks away. Snow drifts were high. People had to wade through the snow to get there.

Oh, how the wind shrieked and howled that night. A voice could scarcely be heard above the noise of the elements. It seemed like the fury of hell had been let loose around us.

I turned to a young man who had travelled with me, and who was mighty in prayer, and said, "Theodore, will you pray?"

He got up and tried to pray, but the wind drowned out his voice, and in a moment he broke down and gave up.

Then, I turned to his wife, Nellie, who was also mighty in prayer, and asked her to lead. She broke, too. All the demons of hell seemed to be let loose on us.

I was walking the platform as Nellie was trying to pray, and when she gave up, I stepped forward and charged the elements in the name of Jesus to cease. I rebuked the storm.

In a moment, it became calm. It wasn't the dying down of the wind. It wasn't the gradual subsiding. It had seemed I couldn't raise my voice above the tumult, and when the storm ceased, before I finished praying, I found that I was actually yelling.

I became quiet. The audience became hushed and awed in the presence and power of that name. It was the name of Jesus.

The text of *We Have Victory in Jesus' Name* is taken from "The Miracle of the Book of John" (unpublished sermon), preached June 1928, 15–16, as quoted in *E. W. Kenyon and His Message of Faith: The True Story* by Joe McIntyre (Lake Mary, FL: Charisma House, 1997), 268–269.

– 30 –
IN THE SECRET OF HIS PRESENCE

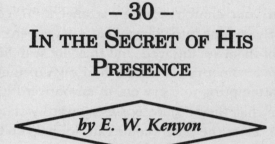

by E. W. Kenyon

There are three prayer problems that I would like to bring to your attention: first, the effective prayer for souls; second, the effective prayer for finances; and third, the sincere bearing of another's burden.

Day after day, you are meeting a never ending stream of people. They are restless and unsettled, searching for something that will satisfy. You can read it in their eyes, hear it in their voices, feel it in their handclasps. You can see it in the very manner in which they walk. You hear your neighbors scolding and fretting with the children, and you notice the worn looks on their faces.

All these things are but manifestations of a deep-seated need for the Son of God; a Savior, a Rest, a Peace, a Strength, a very Quietness that they do not have.

In your church services, strangers are constantly coming into your midst. A large percentage of them are unsaved, and they are searching for that something. Perhaps your own members are attempting to carry on, in an outward way, a life that they do not possess inwardly. Then, from across the waters come calls for help on the mission fields.

Prayer is the only channel. God has shut everything up in prayer. These heartaches and burdens can be met only through prayer. The man or woman who gets down into heart-searching prayer is the channel through whom God can work. The one who takes these burdens and bears them to the Lord in prayer is also the one whom the Lord can trust to go out and speak the necessary word when the time comes. In other words, the one who prays is a personal worker, and the personal worker is by necessity a prayer warrior.

We are daily confronted with financial problems. This may be for the financial needs in the home, in the church, or in the mission field.

God's people are limping along, skimping a little here and stretching a little there to make both ends meet, when God's storehouse is full and running over. There are avenues of endeavor that would mean the carrying of the message to hundreds of thousands of people. The door is standing wide open, and yet the church is too feeble to crawl across the threshold!

Again, the "Why?" is answered in the simple statement that we have failed to pray. We don't need to ask another person to give. We do not need to make public appeals for extra funds. If each person will honestly get down and pray, the money will come in. We have proven it time and again in our ministry.

Here is the secret. If I am honestly giving all that my Lord expects me to give, then I can honestly pray that He will pour out of His abundance. The inward man is conscious of the fact that he cannot hide anything from God. Man may fool man, but there can be no secrets from the Father.

One may rise and publicly address a prayer to the God of the universe, and he may seem very spiritual in the eyes of men, but he knows in his heart whether God hears him or not. This is not a matter in which man can judge man. It is a matter in which each one, in his own heart, must judge himself.

Then, there is the third problem. What do you do when someone asks you to pray for him? Have you promised to pray for individuals and then failed even to remember the request? Have you received their request as a real burden and conveyed that trust to the throne of grace? Have you been faithful to those who have trusted you with their hearts' problems?

The hungry hearts of the unsatisfied are looking to you and expecting results when you pray. The burdened heart of your brother or sister in the Lord expects to feel uplifted, relieved of crushing pressure, when you pray.

We must become real blood covenant men and women and truly share each other's burdens. Dwell in the Word and become a real prayer warrior. Join the prayer ranks. Spend much time in the secret of His presence. Get away to where only the ear of the Father will hear, and, hearing, He will answer.

> *Call unto me, and I will answer thee, and show thee great and mighty things, which thou knowest not.* (Jeremiah 33:3)

– 31 –
SOME FACTS ABOUT HEALING

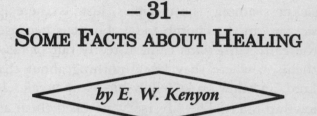

by E. W. Kenyon

From a study of Isaiah 53, it is evident that healing is a part of the plan of redemption. Therefore, the moment that you accept Christ as your Savior and confess Him as your Lord, you have a right to the virtue that is in that redemption, the healing of your sick body.

Healing belongs to every child of God. Some say that it is not the will of God to heal everyone, but there is no scriptural evidence to that effect.

They say, "Didn't Paul have a thorn in the flesh?" Yes, but Paul's thorn in the flesh was not sickness. It came upon Paul because of the exceeding greatness of the revelation that had been given to him. None of us can hide behind that because none of us has ever had a revelation like Paul.

Another says, "Didn't He leave others sick?" Yes, there is no doubt that He did. There was sickness among the disciples, just as there is sickness in the church today, but it is because the early Christians came directly out of heathenism, where they knew nothing about the Lord, and they broke fellowship as we break fellowship today. The adversary attacked them as he attacks us today. If they did not understand their privileges, they might not have known how to maintain their fellowship and health.

We do know that neither Peter nor James nor John ever laid hands upon a person who was not healed. We cannot find a place where it was not the will of God to heal everyone.

I would not argue about it. I would take what belongs to me. I don't love disease enough, and I don't believe that anyone reading this book loves disease and sickness enough to argue the question. I believe we would rather get rid of our troubles.

– 32 –
THE CENTURION'S FAITH

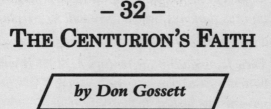

by Don Gossett

When Jesus had entered Capernaum, a centurion came to him, asking for help. "Lord," he said, "my servant lies at home paralyzed and in terrible suffering."

Jesus said to him, "I will go and heal him."

The centurion replied, "Lord, I do not deserve to have you come under my roof. But just say the word, and my servant will be healed. For I myself am a man under authority, with soldiers under me. I tell this one, 'Go,' and he goes; and that one, 'Come,' and he comes. I say to my servant, 'Do this,' and he does it."

When Jesus heard this, he was astonished and said to those following him, "I tell you the truth, I have not found anyone in Israel with such great faith. I say to you that many will

WORDS THAT MOVE MOUNTAINS

come from the east and the west, and will take their places at the feast with Abraham, Isaac and Jacob in the kingdom of heaven. But the subjects of the kingdom will be thrown outside, into the darkness, where there will be weeping and gnashing of teeth."

Then Jesus said to the centurion, "Go! It will be done just as you believed it would." And his servant was healed at that very hour.

(Matthew 8:5–13 NIV)

This is one of my favorite Bible stories. It sets forth all the divine ingredients of triumphant faith—the power of spoken faith in action.

How do you exercise the power of spoken faith? *"The word is nigh thee, even in thy mouth, and in thy heart: that is, the word of faith, which we preach"* (Romans 10:8). It is exercised by believing the Word in your heart and speaking it with your mouth. The centurion of Matthew 8 understood and practiced the power of spoken faith, and Jesus highly commended him. In fact, He called the centurion's faith the greatest faith He had seen in all Israel.

We can speak with the same spirit of faith. *"It is written, I believed, and therefore have I spoken;*

we also believe, and therefore speak" (2 Corinthians 4:13).

Believe and speak. Salvation, the greatest of all God's gifts, comes to us by the believing heart and the confessing mouth. (See Romans 10:9.) When we learn to speak the Word and not the problem, we are on the road to absolute victory. But we are defeated the moment we allow ourselves to start listing our burdens instead of counting our blessings. God bestows His benefits on a daily basis. It should also be a daily matter for us to praise Him.

It would probably surprise us if we knew how much answered prayer depends on our attitude of praise to God. The key to answered requests is that prayer unlocks the door and praise keeps it open. Once we start praising God, we can never really justify stopping, because there is no end to His greatness or to our reasons for being grateful. We all go to Him in prayer, but how many times do we return to praise Him? Remember how Jesus felt about the thankless lepers in Luke 17:

> *And as he entered into a certain village, there met him ten men that were lepers, which stood afar off: And they lifted up their voices, and said, Jesus, Master, have mercy on us. And*

when he saw them, he said unto them, Go show yourselves unto the priests. And it came to pass, that, as they went, they were cleansed. And one of them, when he saw that he was healed, turned back, and with a loud voice glorified God, and fell down on his face at his feet, giving him thanks: and he was a Samaritan. And Jesus answering said, Were there not ten cleansed? but where are the nine? There are not found that returned to give glory to God, save this stranger.   (Luke 17:12–18)

– 33 –
JESUS' AFFIRMATIONS

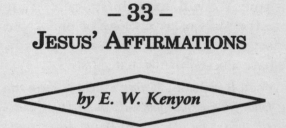

by E. W. Kenyon

Have you ever thought about the fact that Jesus said so many things about Himself? He said, *"I am the way, the truth, and the life: no man cometh unto the Father, but by me"* (John 14:6).

You see, prayer is getting to the Father. Under the first covenant, only the High Priest could get into God's presence—and he only once a year through the Holy of Holies. But now, Jesus has proclaimed, "I am the new way into My Father's presence, and if you will take Me to be your Savior and receive Eternal Life, then you can come through Me into My Father's presence anytime you wish."

The veil that hid the Holy of Holies from the eyes of the people has been rent. Anyone can go into the Holy of Holies now.

Jesus said, "I am the Water of Life. He that drinks of the water that I give will never thirst." (See John 4:14.) We who have drunk know that it is true. We will never thirst again. We don't go to the wells of psychology or philosophy or sensory knowledge and reasoning to get a drink. We have a better drink that satisfies.

When Jesus said, *"I am the light of the world: he that followeth me shall not walk in darkness, but shall have the light of life"* (John 8:12), we don't question it. His affirmations fit into His life. His life and affirmations belong to each other. I know they do, because I have walked in the light of the new kind of life for many years.

Light means wisdom, and Jesus has become our wisdom. He is our light for life's problems. We don't walk in the darkness of sensory knowledge any longer. Once in a while, we lapse down in the valley of sense knowledge, but we grow sick of it at once. Jesus called himself *"the light of life"* (John 8:12).

"I am the bread of life: he that cometh to me shall never hunger" (John 6:35). Once, Jesus said, *"Man shall not live by bread alone, but by every word that proceedeth out of the mouth of God"* (Matthew 4:4). Do you remember how Job said that he fed on the words of God? (See Job 23:12.) Do you

remember how Jeremiah said almost the same thing? (See Jeremiah 15:16.) Well, we have come to feed on this Bread, this Word of God. We know what it means.

Jesus is the solution of the human spirit problem. He answers every cry of our human spirits. Jesus is the solution of life's enigma. He is the Light of life's problems. He is all that the heart could ever ask to know. He satisfies the hungry.

John 6:47 says, *"He that believeth on me hath everlasting life."* You see, what Jesus is saying is, "You believe on Me, you receive Me, and you get eternal life, the nature of God." That fits into the image of Christ, doesn't it? Somehow or other, we can't help but accept it. If anyone else had said it, it wouldn't have meant anything; but He said it, and it means everything.

A dying man once asked me, "Did He say that?" I said, "Yes, sir." He said, "Tell me where it is." And I turned to the Scripture and read it to him.

He said, "I take Him as my Savior. I accept Him as my Lord."

I asked, "Do you have eternal life?" He answered me, "Of course I have. He said it, didn't He?"

I responded, "What do you do when someone gives you something like that?" He replied, "I look up and thank Him for it."

When I left him, he smiled and said, "I have found Him, and I have received Him." That is one of the many affirmations that fit into Jesus' life.

I believe that Jesus is. I believe that He was. I believe that He will be *the same yesterday, and to day, and for ever*" (Hebrews 13:8).

– 34 –
BY YOUR WORDS

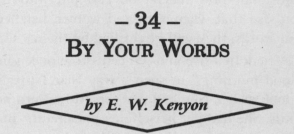

by E. W. Kenyon

Perhaps no one ever told you, but people measure you by your words. You are rated by your words. Your salary is gauged by the value of your words. Your words make a place for you in the business in which you are engaged.

Neither jealousy nor fear can keep you from climbing to the top if your words have value that belongs at the top. The organization is bound to give you the place that belongs to you if your words bring forth the right results.

You don't have to put on; you don't have to exaggerate. All you have to do is to be natural, but make that "natural" worth listening to.

Study your work. Study how to say things. Study how to use words that will change circumstances around you. Make a study, an analytical study of words, then see how much you can put into a single sentence. I don't mean how many words, but how much you can put into the words so that when men and women listen to your words, they will be thrilled by them.

A clerk in a five-and-ten-cent store once said, "Good morning," in such a way that I turned to look at her. She had put something into her words. She had put herself, her personality, into her words. Her words rang. She sold me some pencils at two for five cents, but sold them as though she were selling a Pierce-Arrow car. After I had left the store, I felt inclined to go back and watch her deal with other customers.

Cut out the useless words that stand in the way. Eliminate all the words that would hinder your words from reaching the mark. Trust in words. Trust in the words of your own lips. Fill them with loving truth.

Think in your heart how you want to help those who are to be your customers, how you are going to bless them, and how the thing that you have is necessary to their enjoyment. It is what you put into words that makes them live in the hearts of hearers.

Empty words die in no-man's-land. They never get over the trench. If they do, they are duds. If they do get across and people hear them, they still amount to nothing. Living words—words bursting with heart messages—thrill and grip.

Love always seeks the right word to convey its message without loss of meaning in transit. Clothe your thoughts in the most beautiful words, but don't sacrifice pungency for beauty— blend them.

All He Had Was Words

This is a little study of great things. One man started out in life without sponsors, without a university education, without money. Someone asked him, "What have you beside your two hands to make a success in life?"

He said softly, "I have nothing but words." The friend smiled, not understanding him.

So, he started on his lonely quest for success with nothing but words. He learned the secret of putting things into words, of making words into living things. He loaded his words with thought, clear thought, and, after a bit, he learned the secret of putting his fine, clean, splendid manhood into his words.

Men began to set a value upon his words. People would stop him on the street to engage him in conversation just to hear his words.

You understand that almost every man who has climbed to the top of the ladder of success has climbed there with words.

Here and there, a man has climbed because of an unusual voice or an unusual gift of artistry, but the majority of men have gotten their feet on the first rung of the ladder of success by using words. They climbed, rung by rung, word by word, to the top.

A man must put a valuation on his own words before others will sense their value. The ambitious man's words became his bank account. He studied, he dug deep, he thought through problems. Other people learned to trust his judgment and his words rather than to study for themselves.

There is a vast army of people who have certain business ability, but they have to hire others to do most of their thinking. The ambitious man supplied that want. He did the thinking. By and by, others were willing to pay him almost any price to have him think for them.

His words became valuable. They were his servants. How they labored for him! He filled words with inspiration, with comfort, with hope for others.

By Your Words

He sent them out on wings until they passed from house to house, from lip to lip. He found himself being quoted here and there. His words were doing things. He had learned the secret of words. By and by, publishers paid him unthinkable prices for his words. Why? Because he had learned the art of filling words with inspiration, with new life.

Let's study words. Let's learn to fill them with goodies for the children, healing for the sick, and victory for the discouraged, and we will win.

The text of *By Your Words* is taken from *Signposts on the Road to Success* by E. W. Kenyon (Kenyon's Gospel Publishing Society, 1999), 55–58.

– 35 –
SPEAK THE WORD ONLY

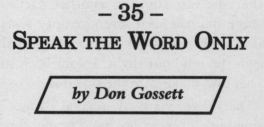

by Don Gossett

I want to share one of the most wonderful testimonies of healing I have ever heard. It happened in a hospital in London, England, in March 1994. I can relate this story perhaps better than anyone else can, because I was deeply involved in it.

My daughter, Judy, and I were traveling in East Africa doing crusades. In Nairobi, Kenya, we had several services every day, and Judy led a hundred-voice choir every night.

Following the crusades in Nairobi, we flew to Mombassa, by the Indian Ocean, for further ministry. The heat and humidity in Mombassa make it one of the most intolerable cities in the world for living accommodations. It was terribly hot, but Judy and I worked very hard while we were there.

Then came the day we were to fly to London for an overnight stay before returning to North America. After we were airborne, Judy told me that she was going to another part of the jet where she had seen several empty seats and could stretch out a bit more. About halfway through the ten-hour flight, I went back to talk with her and make sure she was okay.

"Dad, I've vomited several times," she informed me. I placed my hand on her forehead and prayed a brief, fatherly prayer for her, then returned to my seat. It seemed like something minor; I wasn't overly concerned.

The Crisis

About a half hour before we landed in London, a flight attendant found me and related this grave news.

"Mr. Gossett, I'm sorry to inform you that your daughter, Judy, is a very sick lady. Not only has she vomited many times, she is also hemorrhaging from every opening in her body.

"It is the blood that has us alarmed. We don't know if it's food poisoning or just what the problem is. We have notified Heathrow Airport to meet the flight with a wheelchair for your daughter."

The wheelchair was waiting when we landed, and they took Judy to a medical examining room. After more than an hour, a doctor came out with more critical news: "Mr. Gossett, we have taken blood from your daughter. She has something more severe than parasites, but beyond that we are uncertain. We have ordered an ambulance to come immediately and take her across London to a hospital that specializes in tropical and infectious diseases."

"Please, doctor, that won't be necessary. Judy worked very hard while we were in Africa. I'm sure she will be all right with a good night's rest, and I've booked rooms for us tonight here in London," I explained.

The doctor was quite blunt as she responded to my protest. "Mr. Gossett, leaving the hospital is not an option. Your daughter has been quarantined. She's now the responsibility of British Airways and the city of London. There is no way we would consider permitting her to leave with the highly contagious disease she may have."

At about that time, two men rolled out a stretcher with Judy strapped to it. They told me that I could accompany her to the hospital, so I rode sitting next to Judy in the ambulance.

She looked so weak, especially compared to the strength she usually exudes.

She looked up at me and said, "Dad, I've never been in a hospital a day or night in my life. I wasn't even born in a hospital."

"I know all of that, Judy. But you are going to be all right; God will see you through." I tried to encourage her.

When we arrived at the hospital, a whole battery of doctors and nurses met us. They were all wearing emergency-looking hospital garments, and they quickly took Judy away to an isolation room.

After a long time, Dr. Clark, the chief physician, came out to speak to me.

"Mr. Gossett, your daughter is an extremely ill woman. We will do our best to save her life, but we won't know anything until morning. Meanwhile, you will have to leave the hospital, and you won't be permitted to return until we notify you that you can.

"You may enter the isolation room where your daughter is, but only for twenty minutes. Then you must leave the hospital."

When I was alone with Judy, I told her, "Judy, the doctor has given me only twenty minutes with you before I must leave. We won't have time for deep intercessions for you. But Judy, I'm going to speak the healing Word for you. I have these truths in my spirit—in my 'alphabet of healing.' Remember, Jesus cast out evil spirits with His Word; that's what I'm going to do now. The Word I speak over you will expel these spirits of infirmity and disease. Just receive this Word as I speak it now. Any one of these twenty-six verses can be your healing portion."

I began with the letter **A**:

Attend to my words; incline thine ear unto my sayings. Let them not depart from thine eyes; keep them in the midst of thine heart. For they are life unto those that find them, and health to all their flesh. (Proverbs 4:20–22)

I said, "Judy, His Word is health to all your flesh. This is for you, right now; receive His healing provision for your life!"

Then, I went on to the letter **B**: *"Beloved, I wish above all things that thou mayest prosper and be in health, even as thy soul prospereth"* (3 John 2).

"O beloved Judy, God our Father really wants you to be in health, not in this devastating sickness; it's yours to receive now."

When I spoke the letter **C**, I repeated this

prayer of David: *"Create in me a clean heart, O God; and renew a right spirit within me"* (Psalm 51:10).

I said, "Judy, I believe you have a clean heart and a right spirit. Let's allow the Holy Spirit to do His work of heart-searching and renewal as we yield to Him now."

After Judy and I quietly allowed the Holy Spirit to do His blessed work of cleansing and renewal, we went to the letter **D**: *"Deal bountifully with thy servant, that I may live, and keep thy word"* (Psalm 119:17).

Knowing Judy's very life was at stake, I urgently spoke this letter **D** over her! "That she may live, Lord, and keep Your Word!"

The letter **E**: *"Effectual fervent prayer of a righteous man availeth much"* (James 5:16).

The letter **F** reminded us of God's mercies through the past years: *"Forget not all his benefits: who forgiveth all thine iniquities; who healeth all thy diseases"* (Psalm 103:2–3).

I boldly spoke the letter **G**:

> *God anointed Jesus of Nazareth with the Holy Ghost and with power: who went about doing good, and healing all that were oppressed of the devil; for God was with him.* (Acts 10:38)

When I spoke the letter **H**, I sought to impress

upon Judy this eternal fact: *"He* [Jesus] *took up our infirmities and carried our diseases"* (Matthew 8:17 NIV).

I affirmed that God's original healing covenant was expressed in the letter **I**: *"I am the LORD that healeth thee"* (Exodus 15:26).

Honoring our Lord's majesty came with the letter **J**: *"Jesus Christ the same yesterday, and to day, and for ever"* (Hebrews 13:8).

Next, I spoke the letter **K**:

> *Know ye not that your body is the temple of the Holy Ghost which is in you, which ye have of God, and ye are not your own? For ye are bought with a price: therefore glorify God in your body, and in your spirit, which are God's.* (1 Corinthians 6:19–20)

When I spoke the letter **L**—*"Lay hands on the sick, and they shall recover"* (Mark 16:18), I assured Judy that I would lay hands on her and that Jesus Himself promised she would recover.

M is precious: *"Merry heart doeth good like a medicine"* (Proverbs 17:22).

N magnifies the strong name above all other names:

> [Jesus'] *name through faith in his name hath made this man strong, whom ye see and know:*

yea, the faith which is by him hath given him this perfect soundness in the presence of you all. (Acts 3:16)

The very next day, Judy was to tell me that the letter **O** proved to be the quickening Word, the very rhema of God that ministered healing to her. She declared that after I spoke this letter **O**, she never vomited again, nor did she pass any more blood! What was the dynamic letter **O**?

Ought not this woman, being a daughter of Abraham, whom Satan hath bound, lo, these eighteen years, be loosed from this bond? (Luke 13:16)

I spoke the letter **P**: *"Power of the Lord was present to heal them"* (Luke 5:17).

Q is also precious, honoring the mighty, indwelling Holy Spirit: *"Quicken your mortal bodies by his Spirit that dwelleth in you"* (Romans 8:11).

The letter **R** signifies defeat for the devil: *"Resist the devil, and he will flee from you"* (James 4:7). If we don't resist the devil, he doesn't have to flee. But if we resist him, he must flee!

The letter **S** holds another expression of authority: God *"sent his word, and healed them"* (Psalm 107:20).

Here was **T**: *"Talk ye of all his wondrous works"*

(Psalm 105:2). We talked of His works that night by Judy's bedside.

The letter **U** was next on this alphabet of healing: *"Unto you that fear my name shall the Sun of righteousness arise with healing in his wings"* (Malachi 4:2).

The letter **V** reveals Jesus' active ministry: *"Virtue [went] out of him, and healed them all"* (Luke 6:19).

The letter **W** is, perhaps, the Scripture we have spoken most often for healing: *"With his stripes we are healed"* (Isaiah 53:5).

I spoke the letter **X**: *"Expectation is from him"* (Psalm 62:5).

I assured Judy that the letter **Y** had been good for me for all these years, and it was hers to receive: *"Youth is renewed like the eagle's"* (Psalm 103:5).

I arrived at the final verse of this inspired alphabet, the letter **Z**: *"Zealous of spiritual gifts"* (1 Corinthians 14:12).

When I concluded speaking those twenty-six Bible verses over my daughter, I obeyed the Lord's Word to lay my hands on her for her healing. Then, I had to leave the hospital.

My heart was filled with confidence that the

mighty God was watching over His Word to perform it. (See Jeremiah 1:12.) No word from His mouth would return to Him void of fulfillment (see Isaiah 55:11), because God is not a man that He would lie to us. (See Numbers 23:19.)

The doctor said I could call the next morning. I called at 8:00 AM. "Sorry, Mr. Gossett, we have no information about your daughter to give you now. Call back in another hour," they told me.

I called again at 9:00 AM. Again, the response was the same. "We have no information to give you yet. Call back in another hour."

At 10:00 AM, I called again. The nurse responded, "Right now, twelve doctors are surrounding your daughter's bed. But I have no information to give you. Don't call us again; we'll call you."

I waited patiently in my hotel room, pacing and praising God for the anticipated good report.

When the phone did ring, it was Dr. Clark. He said, "Mr. Gossett, this is remarkable. It's like we have had two different women in that bed. Last night when we took blood, results showed that the infection was severe. We gave her no medicine, because we didn't know how to medicate her.

"This morning we took blood again. Now her blood is completely clean and pure! We have just now discharged your daughter from this hospital. We will be putting her in a taxi for the trip to Heathrow Airport. She will be joining you for your flight back to America this afternoon!"

I was practically shouting praises to the Lord! I quickly packed my bag and checked out of the hotel. I boarded a bus to take me to Heathrow Airport, but in my excitement, I got on the wrong bus and had to get back off again. When I finally arrived at Heathrow, Judy was waiting for me!

If you need healing, I recommend that you affirm all twenty-six of the Bible verses listed in this chapter. They contain God's healing provisions for your spirit, soul, and body. Believe and receive your healing!

– 36 –
HOW I FOUND IT

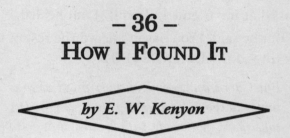

by E. W. Kenyon

I had been afflicted for years with a nervous trouble. At times it was so unbearable that it seemed as though I would lose my mind. Then, one day, I was visiting a friend of mine who knew the Word, and I told him about my affliction.

He said, "Have you ever read Isaiah 53:4–5?"

"Why, I know that Scripture and have known it since I was a child." I recited it to him:

> *Surely he hath borne our griefs, and carried our sorrows: yet we did esteem him stricken, smitten of God, and afflicted. But he was wounded for our transgressions, he was bruised for our iniquities: the chastisement of our peace was upon him; and with his stripes we are healed.*

I knew the Scripture, but it had not meant

anything to me. Now, my friend went over it, and I listened to every word. It troubled me. I wondered why I had never seen it before. I looked at my friend and said, "I am healed."

But he said, "You haven't heard the rest of it." He turned to Hebrews 9:11–12.

> *But Christ being come an high priest of good things to come, by a greater and more perfect tabernacle, not made with hands, that is to say, not of this building; neither by the blood of goats and calves, but by his own blood he entered in once into the holy place, having obtained eternal redemption for us.*

And I saw that Christ had entered into the Holy Place with His own blood, and that the Supreme Court of the Universe had accepted that blood as the red seal upon the eternal document of my redemption.

I turned back to Hebrews 1:3:

> *Who being the brightness of his glory, and the express image of his person, and upholding all things by the word of his power, when he had by himself purged our sins, sat down on the right hand of the Majesty on high.*

And in Hebrews 9:24:

*For Christ is not entered into the holy places
made with hands, which are the figures of the
true; but into heaven itself, now to appear in
the presence of God for us.*

I saw it. I saw Christ seated there on the right
hand of the Father. And in Hebrews 7:25:

*Wherefore he is able also to save them to the
uttermost that come unto God by him, seeing
he ever liveth to make intercession for them.*

Then, I understood Hebrews 9:26: *"But now
once in the end of the world hath he appeared to put
away sin."* He not only put away sin, but He also
put away my old man, all my old diseases. He
put away everything bad that had ever touched
my life.

Then, my friend asked, "Have you ever
noticed Ephesians 1?"

"Why, I know Ephesians 1 by heart."

But when he opened it up to me, I saw what
I had never seen before. Let us begin with the
seventeenth verse:

*That the God of our Lord Jesus Christ, the
Father of glory, may give unto you the spirit
of wisdom and revelation in the knowledge of
him.*

Then, I saw that I had lacked a knowledge of Him. I had not realized what He had done and how complete and perfect was the work that He had wrought on my behalf. I had not realized the significance of the new creation created in Christ Jesus. I now saw for the first time that I was a perfectly recreated being, that the old things that had held me in bondage had passed away, and that the new things of light and life and love had taken their place.

Then, I began to understand what it meant to have the *"eyes of* [my] *understanding being enlightened; that* [I] *may know what is the hope of his calling, and...the riches of the glory of his inheritance in* [me]" (Ephesians 1:18). I had never thought of that. God had an inheritance in me. I had never realized that He had an inheritance that, in His estimation, was rich and full of glory in me.

And next, He wanted me to know the exceeding greatness of His power on my behalf as a believer. He said that it was according to the riches of His might that He wrought in Christ His resurrection from the dead. In other words, the very ability that was at work in Jesus is mine.

Then, I saw in Ephesians 1:20–23 that,

[God caused Christ to sit] *at his own right hand in the heavenly places, far above all principality, and power, and might, and dominion, and every name that is named, not only in this world, but also in that which is to come: And hath put all things under his feet, and gave him to be the head over all things to the church, which is his body, the fulness of him that filleth all in all.*

Then, Ephesians 2:6 reached out and grasped my heart: *"And* [He] *hath raised* [me] *up together; and made* [me] *sit* [with Him] *in heavenly places in Christ Jesus."* I saw that I was identified with Him, that I was actually seated with Him in that place of authority, and I saw that I was a master of demons; I was a master of disease in that name.

You see, He gave unto Him the name that is above every name; of the beings on the earth, under the earth, and above the earth. (See Philippians 2:9–10.) In those three worlds, every being is subject to that name, and now He gives me the power of attorney to use that name, too.

He has made me a master, and I am to represent Him in the world. I can't represent Him if the devil is my master, or if my body is full of disease. But now I see that disease has been put away.

He has made me His righteousness in Christ. He has not only made me His righteousness, but He also has given me the authority that is represented in His name.

God was saying, in effect, "Now go and make disciples of all nations. I have empowered you. I have given you My ability. You can laugh at the enemy because Christ is made unto you the wisdom from God. You have wisdom greater than the adversary's wisdom and ability that is greater than the adversary's ability. You are a master today. I am in you, and I am greater."

I saw it, and I said, "Satan, have you heard these Scriptures? Do you see what I know now? You are defeated. I am a conqueror. I am a master now. If I were in your place, I would clear out now!"

Now I walk by faith—faith in the Son of God who loved me and gave Himself up for me. I have come to see that we are one.

– 37 –
MY CONFESSION

by E. W. Kenyon

Our words give us our standing among men. In the same way, our words give us a standing with the adversary and with the Word.

If, as a child of God, I make a confession of sickness and failure, I go to the level of that confession. If I always confess victory and perfect health and proclaim that my needs are met, I go to the level of that confession.

Here is a little confession that I wrote out. I have never read it to anyone before, but I am going to print it here for you.

My Father, through Jesus Christ, Your Son, I have received eternal life, Your nature. It has made me one with You. It has made me what You have declared that I am in Christ. As the branch is to the vine, I am Yours and You are mine.

My heart sings this song of utter oneness with You, my Father; of my utter oneness with You, my Lord.

Your nature is love, so my nature is love. Out from my inner being flows love to all mankind. I am, like You, a lover. Through me, this love-stream flows unhindered.

You are the fountain within me, a fountain of perfect health and vibrant life. This life-stream fills me with health and joy. My body is Your home, one of the Holy of Holies where You are not hidden, but made visible. It is the home of health, the home of love. You have made Him, my risen Lord, my Wisdom.

At last I know how to use revelation knowledge. I know how to use sense knowledge. My union with You makes me a master of circumstance, for I have learned how to let You have Your freedom in me, let You put Your very self in me. This has freed me from the old realm of fear and doubt.

Jesus has given me the power of attorney,

a legal right to use His name, so that I can act for Him, take His place, do the work that He did, and carry on the works He started. Your ability has become my ability. Your grace has taken me over. I am the slave of Your love. It has over-mastered me, and I have become a love-slave of Your Son. You are living in me and through me. Your life and Your love nature dominate me. You are the strength of my life.

This life is like a fountain within me. I remember what the Master said in John 7:38, that out from my inner life shall gush torrents of living water. This has been my dream: that I might be a little fountain through which You can pour Your very life daily through me to bless this arid desert world.

I have come to know the reality of the verse, *"greater is he that is in you, than he that is in the world"* (1 John 4:4). You mighty Lover God, I give You Your place in me. You mighty Father God, do Your creative work through me. Be unhindered in my life.

What grace You have unveiled to let me use Your living Word! In my lips, Your words become healing words, faith-giving words, and life-giving words!

Arise, my Father, and be big in me! How many times my heart has cried that You might be a God-sized God in me so that You could pour Your very self through me in words and actions, that every part of my being would be under Your direction.

I do not ask for healing, for by His stripes I am healed. I do not ask for strength, because He is the strength of my life. I do not ask to be filled, for He is my fullness. I do not ask for righteousness, because I am His righteousness in Christ. I do not ask for power, as He is in me and all power is in me now. I am planning on His ability in me, on His love nature governing me, and on His wisdom as a lamp to guide me into all truth.

I am letting You loose in me. I am letting You use my abilities, speak through my lips, and heal through my hands.

I am filled with Your fullness. Your wisdom and love are mine. Love's gentleness and greatness are all mine. Your own tender steadfastness has become a part of me. I am resting in Your rest. Your very peace holds me quiet. I am Yours, and You are mine. Life is big with You in it.

AFTERWORD

by Don Gossett

I am watching to see that my word is fulfilled.
—Jeremiah 1:12 (NIV)

When our words are in agreement with God's Word, we experience the continual manifestation of God's blessing. With faith and affirmative confession, our words can change lives and move mountains! (See Matthew 21:21.)

Here are just a few of the "word victories" I've known after walking with God by agreeing with God.

► *"Can two walk together, except they be agreed?"* (Amos 3:3).

► Only eighteen months after we lost a home by repossession, the Lord provided us a wonderful new home in Surrey.

▶ The Lord put me on international radio, and the finances have come in, month after month, for more than forty years now.

▶ The Lord removed a cancerous growth from my head just hours before my scheduled surgery.

▶ When I was a lonely man after the death of Joyce, my dear first wife, in 1991, God brought sweet and delightful Debra to become my wife. Again, I must say, "Praise to the Lord" ten times!

▶ The Lord led Whitaker House to begin publishing my books, eventually even translating them into many other languages.

▶ After reading my book *What You Say Is What You Get*, the men of World Harvesters in New Jersey invited me to be an evangelist for great crusades in India. More than two hundred thousand were reported "saved by grace through faith" (see Ephesians 2:8) in the first three crusades.

▶ I was invited to preach to eighty-nine

nations through Trans World Radio, originating from Monte Carlo, on a superpower station originally built for Hitler to proclaim Nazism.

▶ God gave me total healing from violent headaches, climaxed by a personal visit from an angel of the Lord. Precious experience! That was in 1976, and I would be the most surprised person if I ever suffered from another headache after that Word victory.

▶ To the best of my memory, I have never in fifty-three years missed a preaching assignment because of ill health. By the grace of God, I never have to miss "life abundant" because of having to take a day off for sickness.

▶ As I narrated earlier, when my daughter, Judy, was stricken with a rare blood disease, the spoken Word caused the deadly sickness to vanish from her body, and her life was saved. Praise the Lord!

Words work wonders! Words can move mountains! Words that agree with God's Word will never return void.

*My word…that goeth forth out of my mouth…
shall not return unto me void, but it shall accomplish that which I please, and it shall prosper in
the thing whereto I sent it.*   (Isaiah 55:11)

Tribute to E. W. Kenyon

Pastor George Hunter was a close associate of Dr. E. W. Kenyon and most likely the author of the following tribute, written in November of 1930. He knew firsthand the triumphs and trials of Kenyon's life, and his words are filled with love and care. His message touched my heart. I pray it will likewise minister to you.

—*Don Gossett*

Mountains and Valleys

No man that we know of has such a gift as a teacher. We all wonder at him, but let us remember the price he has had to pay.

I have seen Dr. Kenyon suffer as few men have suffered.

During those early days at Bible school, the things I saw him pass through are almost unbelievable. I saw him suffer persecution from brethren. I remember the early struggles against false teachings. I saw him suffer financial loss and misunderstanding. I saw the work of false friends. I saw those he helped, turn traitor. I knew of heartaches unknown to the crowds. Then I saw sickness and death come and take his mate [she died in 1914]. I stood at the graveside with him. I saw men rob him of all he had labored for. Lies, abuse, and insults were heaped upon him, and in the midst of it all, he walked like a king, and God gave him victory in his soul.

I have also seen him enjoy happy days and prosperity, without losing his head.

I remember the high spots in his life—when a great Bible school was in full swing; when evangelistic tours were winning thousands; when the country was praising him; when he again took a bride to himself and had a happy home; when he enjoyed the love of a great body of young ministers whom he had trained.

Mountains and valleys, one after another, have all worked together to make the teacher what he is today.

The text of *Mountains and Valleys* is taken from a Figueroa Independent Baptist Church bulletin (1930), as quoted in *E. W. Kenyon and His Message of Faith: The True Story* by Joe McIntyre (Lake Mary, FL: Charisma House, 1997), 153–154.

TRIBUTE TO DON GOSSETT

A Daughter's Perspective
by Judy Gossett

This morning while watching television, I observed several famous evangelists: Oral Roberts, Rex Humbard, and Robert Schuller. It was quite interesting to note the participation and support of their children in their religious ministries. It seems as though a chief accomplishment for each of these great men was to have their own flesh and blood actively involved with them, endorsing them, believing in and wholeheartedly supporting the work God has called their fathers to.

On behalf of the five Gossett children, I want to pay tribute to our father, Don Gossett.

One of the most striking memories I carry from childhood is we seven Gossetts—Dad, Mom, Michael, Jeanne, Donnie, Marisa, and me—packed into our blue '56 Buick, driving from one city to the next in our evangelistic travels. As we grew restless and tired of playing our children's games in the tight quarters of our old car, Dad would announce, "Okay, kids, it's Bible story time!" As Dad recounted thrilling stories from the Old and New Testaments, we became mesmerized by each event and character, feeling sure that at any moment, Moses would put in a cameo appearance, complete with the Ten Commandments in hand, or that we were trekking the water beside Peter as Jesus directed! These were fascinating, vibrant stories, and we devoured them.

Bible quizzes, "sword drills," and Scripture memorization followed the Bible story time. We children preferred the time spent in the Word with our parents to any other activity of our journeys. Thankfully, many times, the Lord has brought to my remembrance the Scriptures and lessons learned in those long hours in our car. These have been invaluable in building the spiritual character and witness needed to be effective for Christ.

Because we traveled so much, it was difficult for us to establish long-term relationships with the people we met. As a result, our family grew closer than ever.

Many afternoons, we played sports outside

our motel room—lively games of baseball adn touch football—or rivaled each other in endurance-testing races and swimming. Usually in the middle of the jovial festivities was our favorite competitor and coach: Dad.

In spite of the deep love and devotion in our family, it seemed as though we were constantly plagued with near-poverty, sickness, mediocrity, and frustration.

Then, in 1961, we moved back to Canada, and the Lord turned around Dad's ministry. God showed Dad that the power of Jesus' name, coupled with positive confession of the Word and joyful praise, were the keys to success and victorious living. These truths revolutionized our lives! We could never again live in the defeatism of past years in the ministry.

As we grew older, Dad and Mom experienced more problems with us as teenagers. However, they never shirked from these obstacles but always met them head-on with these responses: discipling, the Word, the name of Jesus, and prayer. Michael, Jeanne, Donnie, Marisa, and I aren't perfect, but we do possess a wonderful heritage from our persevering, confident-through-Christ parents. And now with Jeanne's children, Jennifer and Alexander, another generation is receiving the same truths we were taught years ago.

These have been exciting years for Dad's ministry. The Lord opened the doors for the Bold Living radio broadcasts to beam into eighty-nine countries. God increased Dad's visibility as an author and gave him more than eighty books to publish. We opened offices in both Canada and the States to service the needs of the partners God raised up to support the various outreaches of the ministry. Dad has gone overseas more than forty times to spread the good news of Jesus' love with those who have never heard.

Perhaps you have always heard of Don Gossett as an evangelist, radio speaker, administrator, author, or missionary.

By way of this brief personal glimpse, I hope you know him a little better as a compassionate man of God, loving father, proud grandfather, and my wonderful friend.

ABOUT E. W. KENYON

Born in Saratoga county, New York, E. W. Kenyon (1867–1948) moved with his family to Amsterdam, New York, when he was in his teens. Kenyon studied at Amsterdam Academy, and, at the age of nineteen, preached his first sermon in the Methodist church there.

He worked his way through school, attending various schools in New Hampshire, as well as Emerson College of Oratory in Boston, Massachusetts.

Kenyon served as pastor of several churches in the New England states. At the age of thirty, he founded and became president of Bethel Bible Institute in Spencer, Massachusetts. (This school was later moved to Providence, Rhode Island, and is known as Providence Bible Institute.) Through his ministry at Bethel, hundreds of young men and women were trained and ordained for the ministry.

After traveling throughout the Northeast preaching the gospel and seeing the salvation and healing of thousands, Kenyon moved to California, where he continued his evangelistic travels. He was pastor of a church in Los Angeles for several years and was one of the pioneers of radio work on the Pacific Coast.

In 1931, he moved to the Northwest, and for many years his morning broadcast, *Kenyon's Church of the Air,* was an inspiration and blessing to thousands. He also founded the New Covenant Baptist Church in Seattle, where he pastored for many years.

During the busy years of his ministry, he found time to write and publish sixteen books, as well as many correspondence courses and tracts, and he composed hundreds of poems and songs. The work that he started has continued to bless untold thousands.

ABOUT DON GOSSETT

For more than fifty years, Don Gossett has been serving the Lord through full-time ministry. Born again at the age of twelve, Don answered his call to the ministry just five years later, beginning by reaching out to his unsaved family members. In March 1948, Don overcame his longtime fear of public speaking and began his ministry in earnest, preaching for two country Baptist churches in Oklahoma.

Blessed with the gift of writing, Don became editor of the Bible College magazine in San Francisco; afterward, he was invited to become editor of an international magazine. Following this, he served as editor of T. L. Osborn's *Faith Digest*, a magazine that reached over 600,000 homes each month. Don apprenticed with many well-known evangelists, beginning with William Freeman, one of America's leading healing evangelists during the late 1940s. He also spent time with Jack Coe and Raymond T. Richey.

Don has penned many works, particularly ones on the power of the spoken word and praise. His writings have been translated into almost twenty languages and have exceeded twenty-five million in worldwide distribution. Additionally, Don has also recorded scores of audio series. His daily radio broadcast, launched in 1961, has been released into eighty-nine nations worldwide.

Don raised five children with his first wife, Joyce, who died in 1991. In 1995, Don found life-long love again and married Debra, an anointed teacher of the Word. They have ministered worldwide and have lived in British Columbia, Canada, and in Blaine, Washington State.

There's Dynamite in Praise
Don Gossett

Praise can bring life where there was death, freedom where there was bondage, and divine joy where there was sorrow. When you learn to praise God at all times and in all circumstances, you will experience a truly victorious life, and He will work wonders on your behalf. Don Gossett helps you to discover the tremendous power that awaits you in learning to praise the Lord!

ISBN: 978-0-88368-644-7 • Trade • 128 pages

WHITAKER
HOUSE

WHAT YOU SAY
IS WHAT YOU GET!

DON GOSSETT

NATIONAL BEST SELLER

What You Say Is What You Get
Don Gossett

This best-selling book reveals the power of our
words when we proclaim them in agreement with
what the Word of God declares. Don Gossett's
fresh and uplifting message of faith and hope will
teach you how to receive healing, wisdom, answers
to prayer, and much more! Discover the key to
peace, love, joy, prosperity, happiness, and health.

ISBN: 978-0-88368-066-7 • Mass Market • 224 pages

WHITAKER
HOUSE

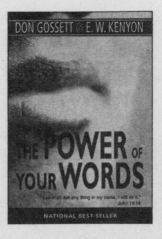

The Power of Your Words
Don Gossett & E. W. Kenyon

If you lack anything or fail to accomplish what you say
you will do, then the problem may be in what you are
confessing. Discover how to gain mastery over the
words coming out of your mouth so they line up with
God's Word, and learn to hold fast to your confession
of faith even in the face of apparent contradictions.
With dynamic chapters written by E. W. Kenyon and
Don Gossett, this book helps you to realize there is
nothing that equals *The Power of Your Words*!

ISBN: 978-0-88368-348-4 • Mass Market • 224 pages

WHITAKER
HOUSE